Florida Benchmark and Unit Tests

Grade 3

Photo Credits

38 ©Image Source/Getty Images; 39 ©Image Source/Getty Images; 103 Malcolm Fife/Photodisc/Getty Images; 174 Elena Elisseeva/Alamy

Printed in the U.S.A.

ISBN 978-0-547-86683-3

3 4 5 6 7 8 9 10 0982 21 20 19 18 17 16 15 14 13

4500414263 A B C D E F G

Contents

Unit 1 Benchmark Test **1–35**
Reading and Analyzing Text 1–26
Revising and Editing 27–32
Writing to Narrate 33–35
Unit 1 Performance Task (Reading Complex Text) **37–40**
Unit 2 Unit Test **41–69**
Reading and Analyzing Text 41–58
Revising and Editing 59–64
Writing Opinions 65–69
Unit 2 Performance Task (Reading Complex Text) **71–74**
Unit 3 Benchmark Test **75–108**
Reading and Analyzing Text 75–99
Revising and Editing 100–105
Writing to Inform 106–108
Unit 3 Performance Task (Reading Complex Text) **109–112**
Unit 4 Unit Test **113–139**
Reading and Analyzing Text 113–130
Revising and Editing 131–136
Writing Opinions 137–139
Unit 4 Performance Task (Reading Complex Text) **141–143**
Unit 5 Benchmark Test **145–179**
Reading and Analyzing Text 145–167
Revising and Editing 168–176
Writing to Narrate 177–179
Unit 5 Performance Task (Reading Complex Text) **181–184**

Unit 6 Unit Test **185–212**
Reading and Analyzing Text 185–200
Revising and Editing 201–209
Writing to Inform 210–212
Unit 6 Performance Task (Reading Complex Text) **213–216**
Unit 6 Novel Tests 217–225
Donavan's Word Jar 217–219
Jake Drake, Know-It-All 220–222
Capoeira 223–225

Name Brendan Date

Reading and Analyzing Text

Read the story "The Color Wheel" before answering Numbers 1 through 6.

The Color Wheel

Jaden and Noah were planning to redecorate their bedroom. The brothers were quite excited and ready to make changes, but mostly, they were eager to start painting.

"It's going to look so awesome with green walls," said Jaden.

"What? Who said anything about green walls?" Noah argued. "I was planning to paint our room red."

"Red will look horrible, and besides, green is a much better color," Jaden replied.

The boys' smiles disappeared, and frowns started to become visible.

"Okay, let's think about this. I'm sure we can decide on a color together," said Noah.

"Hey, I have an idea that might be useful. Our art teacher showed us how to use a color wheel, which displays all of the colors of the rainbow. All of the colors are arranged in a circle, and the color wheel shows how new colors are made from mixing certain main colors together. Let's look at a color wheel and see what we can come up with," Jaden suggested.

Jaden pulled out a book about art that included a color wheel.

"How is that going to help us?" Noah asked.

"Well, maybe we'll find another color we both like," Jaden answered.

Jaden opened the book to a page with a color wheel on it, and the boys began to study it. They saw that red and green are on opposite sides of the color wheel, which means they are very different from one another. Sometimes colors that are not alike work well together, but they can also be so different that they don't work well together.

Name ______________________ Date ____________

"Hey, these colors look good together," said Jaden. He pointed to a golden color and a green color. The colors were side by side on the color wheel, but they were not similar.

Noah agreed. "But I really do like red," he added.

"Well, I like blue as much as I like green. What would happen if we mixed blue and red?" Jaden asked.

The boys looked at the color wheel. The color in between red and blue on the wheel was purple. They looked at each other and started to grin.

"I think we might have solved our problem," said Jaden.

"I think you're right," said Noah.

Name _______________ Date _______

Now answer Numbers 1 through 6. Base your answers on the story "The Color Wheel."

1 What is the story MOSTLY about?

Ⓐ two brothers who cannot get along

Ⓑ two brothers who cannot make a decision

Ⓒ two brothers who discuss a problem and work it out

Ⓓ two brothers who decide to paint a bedroom two colors

2 Read this sentence from the story.

The brothers were quite excited and ready to make changes, but mostly, they were eager to start painting.

Which word means the OPPOSITE of the word *eager* in the sentence above?

Ⓕ annoyed

Ⓖ ready

Ⓗ thoughtless

Ⓘ unwilling

3 Why does Jaden suggest that he and Noah look at a color wheel?

Ⓐ to find a color they both like

Ⓑ to prove green is better than red

Ⓒ to make Noah forget about the problem

Ⓓ to show Noah what he learned in school

Name _______________ Date _______________

4 Which of the following do BOTH Jaden and Noah agree about in the story?

- Ⓕ Red and green look good together.
- Ⓖ Green and gold look good together.
- Ⓗ Red is the best color to paint the walls.
- Ⓘ Blue is the best color to paint the walls.

5 Which message can BEST be learned from the story?

- Ⓐ Some problems cannot be solved.
- Ⓑ It is important to always prove you are right.
- Ⓒ Meeting in the middle can solve an argument.
- Ⓓ Family members often have the same opinions.

6 Which conclusion can BEST be drawn at the end of the story?

- Ⓕ Noah and Jaden will paint their bedroom purple.
- Ⓖ Noah and Jaden will decide on a color another day.
- Ⓗ Noah and Jaden will keep looking at the color wheel.
- Ⓘ Noah and Jaden will paint their bedroom blue and red.

Read the article "Animal Homes" before answering Numbers 7 through 12.

Animal Homes

Some animals live in open areas. When they get tired, they just lie down to sleep. Other animals use caves or hollowed-out trees as their homes. Various animals are able to build their own homes. Beavers, prairie dogs, alligators, and hornets all build their own places to live.

Beavers

Beavers build a home called a lodge. Beavers move slowly on land but are quick in the water. So, they build their homes in water to stay safe. Beavers use their four long, sharp front teeth to cut down trees. They use trees and branches to make a dam. The dam blocks the flow of water in a stream and creates a pond. Then beavers build their lodge, which looks like a mountain of sticks and mud, in the pond. Other animals are unable to get inside the lodge because the entrance is under the water. Inside the lodge, the beavers are safe and sound, with a dry place to sleep and eat.

Prairie Dogs

Another animal that builds its home is the prairie dog. Prairie dogs are members of the squirrel family, but they do not live in trees. These animals dig tunnels for a place to live. They make what is called a town, which is made of many tunnels and small rooms. Hundreds of prairie dogs live in the town together. They carry grass inside to make comfortable beds. Prairie dogs are secure in their towns because large animals cannot get inside. The towns stay cool on hot days. They also stay warm when it is cold outside.

Alligators

Alligators build homes called nests. An alligator nest is built at the edge of the water. It is made of grass and mud. Some nests are about three feet high and six feet wide. The female alligator lays her eggs in the nest, which is a very special place because it is built to keep the eggs warm. The female covers the eggs with rotting plants. These rotting plants make heat.

Name ______________________ Date ____________

Hornets

Another animal that makes its home in a nest is the hornet. Hornets are flying insects, much like bees. Hornets make big, round nests that look like gray balloons. The hornets make the nest by chewing wood that becomes soft and wet. After the pieces of wood dry, they become paper. Inside the nest, there are tiny cups. The eggs and the young hornets stay in these cups.

Animals' homes keep them safe, warm, and dry. Animals build homes for many of the same reasons that people build homes!

Now answer Numbers 7 through 12. Base your answers on the article "Animal Homes."

7 Read this sentence from the story.

Some animals live in open areas.

If the word *animal* means "a living organism," then what does the word *animated* mean?

- Ⓐ large
- Ⓑ lazy
- Ⓒ lively
- Ⓓ organized

Name ______________________ Date __________

8 Read this sentence from the article.

Then beavers build their lodge, which looks like a mountain of sticks and mud, in the pond.

Why does the author compare a beaver's lodge to a mountain in the sentence above?

Ⓕ to show how high they build the lodge

Ⓖ to show where the lodge is in the pond

Ⓗ to show that other animals cannot climb it

Ⓘ to show what types of sticks and mud they use

9 How do beavers prevent other animals from getting inside their lodges?

Ⓐ They build the entrance under water.

Ⓑ They use trees to block the entrance.

Ⓒ They build lodges in fast-flowing water.

Ⓓ They plug the entrance with sticks and mud.

10 Read this sentence from the article.

Inside the lodge, the beavers are safe and sound, with a dry place to sleep and eat.

What does the phrase *safe and sound* mean in the sentence above?

Ⓕ friendly

Ⓖ protected

Ⓗ quiet

Ⓘ strong

Name ______________________ Date ______________

11 Read this sentence from the article.

Prairie dogs are secure in their towns because large animals cannot get inside.

What does the word *secure* mean in the sentence above?

Ⓐ calm

Ⓑ locked

Ⓒ safe

Ⓓ warm

12 Why does the female alligator cover her eggs with rotting plants?

Ⓕ to keep the eggs hidden

Ⓖ to help keep the eggs warm

Ⓗ to provide food for her young

Ⓘ to help her remember where her nest is

Read the story "New Kitten" before answering Numbers 13 through 17.

New Kitten

by Mona Pease
art by Helen Cogancherry

I have a new kitten. He lives at my grandparents' house, but I visit him every weekend.

When Grandma told me I could have a kitten, we went shopping for things it would need. We bought a litter box and litter, a soft brush, and some dry kitten food. I picked out a fluffy mouse and a small ball, too. Grandma and Grandpa took me to their neighbors' farm to pick a kitten from their mother cat's litter.

There were four kittens left. They were all so cute that we couldn't decide which one to choose, so we stood very still and waited to see which kitten would come to us. A tiger-striped one climbed on my shoe and meowed. We brought him home, and I named him Jethro.

Name ______________________ Date ______________

When I picked Jethro up, he purred really loudly. At first, I thought it was his stomach growling! He didn't want to snuggle too long. He wanted to play. He let me carry him around in a basket. Then he played with his ball and batted at his toy mouse. Soon he got tired and fell asleep.

Grandma told me that I would take care of Jethro on weekends. Grandma said she would keep the litter box clean, but the rest was up to me. It was my job to keep Jethro's dishes clean and filled with fresh water and food. She said another job was to gently brush him to keep his coat from getting snarled. I promised to take good care of my kitten.

One day Grandma and I took Jethro to the veterinarian. That's a special doctor for animals, just like my pediatrician is a special doctor for children. In the car, Jethro rode in a small carrier that looked like a cage. Even though Grandma had put his little mouse inside, Jethro didn't like being closed in. He yowled all the way! When we got to the veterinarian's office, Grandma filled out a paper that told the workers Jethro's name and age and who owned him. She put my name on that line.

The veterinarian listened to Jethro's heart with her stethoscope. She looked at his eyes and in his ears. Uh-oh! She said my kitten had ear mites and gave us some medicine to take home. And then, just like at my pediatrician's, Jethro needed a shot. It was to keep him from getting any bad cat diseases. Jethro meowed, so I guess he didn't like that very much.

Now Jethro is home, and Grandpa puts the medicine in his ears every day.

Grandma cleans the litter box, and I wash Jethro's dishes and make sure they're full of food and water. I don't mind all the work I have to do for him, because I love my kitten.

Now answer Numbers 13 through 17. Base your answers on the story "New Kitten."

13 Why does the narrator pick Jethro to take home from the farm?

Ⓐ Jethro is the biggest of all the kittens.

Ⓑ Jethro is the first kitten to come forward.

Ⓒ Jethro is the best-behaved of all the kittens.

Ⓓ Jethro is the only kitten that has tiger-stripes.

14 What happens when it is discovered that Jethro has ear mites?

Ⓕ Jethro gets medicine.

Ⓖ Jethro's heart is checked.

Ⓗ Jethro's eyes are checked.

Ⓘ Jethro is put in his carrier.

15 Read the dictionary entry below.

shot \shŏt\ *noun* **1.** an injection of medicine. **2.** a chance or a try; a guess. **3.** an attempt to reach a target.

Read this sentence from the story.

> **And then, just like at my pediatrician's, Jethro needed a shot.**

Which meaning BEST fits the way the word *shot* is used in the sentence above?

Ⓐ meaning 1

Ⓑ meaning 2

Ⓒ meaning 3

Ⓓ meaning 4

Name _______________ Date _______________

16 How does the picture on page 10 help the reader understand how the narrator feels about Jethro?

Ⓕ It shows why he wants Jethro.

Ⓖ It shows how caring he is toward Jethro.

Ⓗ It shows how worried he is about Jethro.

Ⓘ It shows how amazing he thinks Jethro is.

17 Which word BEST describes Grandma in the story?

Ⓐ careful

Ⓑ playful

Ⓒ funny

Ⓓ loving

Name ______________________ Date ____________

Read the story "Friends Go Shopping" before answering Numbers 18 through 23.

Friends Go Shopping

Sonja, Urie, and Gabrielle were shopping with Urie's mom at the mall one day. They always enjoyed each other's company when strolling through the stores and daydreaming about wearing the newest fashions. There was one catch today, though. They had only five dollars each to spend.

The girls were eager to take a peek at the jewelry store, the music store, and the many other interesting shops in the mall. They couldn't help dashing across the mall and through the stores. Urie told her friends that she was starting to get hungry. They headed over to the food court, where a variety of snacks were available. Soon, most of their money was gone.

After lunch, the girls continued shopping. As Sonja passed a clothing store, she stopped suddenly, and Urie and Gabrielle turned to look at Sonja. "What is it, Sonja?" asked Gabrielle.

"That sweater in the store window," answered Sonja, "I just have to get it!"

"I bet that style would look amazing on you," said Urie, "and it looks like the store carries one in your favorite color!"

"I know. I love that shade of purple," said Sonja. "I've been hunting for one just like it for months!" Sonja rushed into the store and tried the sweater on, hoping it would fit. The sweater fit perfectly. But the price was more than Sonja could afford.

Sonja remembered shopping with her mother a few months ago. Sonja's mother had wanted to buy a dress that she had tried on. But the store had only one dress in her size, and it had a large smear of dirt on the collar. When Sonja's mother brought the soiled dress to the salesclerk's attention, he had given her a discount. Sonja's mother bought the dress at a reduced price, and she had removed the stain at home.

Sonja examined the sweater for flaws, but she didn't find any stains or tears. "What if I 'accidentally' got lipstick on this?" Sonja wondered. "Would I get a discount, too? But that would be dishonest," she said to herself, as she reluctantly put the sweater back on the clothing rack and joined her friends.

"I need to talk to you two," she said. "I really need your opinion. I want that sweater, but I don't have enough money to buy it." Sonja quickly told her friends about her mother's dress. "I'm tempted to get it dirty and ask for a discount. What do you think?"

"Sonja, that's not like you," Gabrielle said, frowning. "Why don't you just wait until you have the money?"

"But how would I ever get enough money to buy that sweater?" asked Sonja.

"You can do extra chores at home," answered Urie. "If you save all of your money, you'll have enough in no time."

Sonja looked at the sweater and then turned back to her friends. "You're right. I can earn the money if I work hard. I'm lucky to have friends who always remind me of the right thing to do!"

Name ______________________ Date ____________

Now answer Numbers 18 through 23. Base your answers on the story "Friends Go Shopping."

18 Where does MOST of this story take place?

Ⓕ in a bookstore

Ⓖ in a food court

Ⓗ in a music store

Ⓘ in a clothing store

19 Read this sentence from the story.

"I've been hunting for one just like it for months!"

Why does the author use the word *hunting* in the sentence above?

Ⓐ to show that Sonja isn't sure she wants to spend her money on a sweater

Ⓑ to show that Sonja's friends think Sonja would look nice in a purple sweater

Ⓒ to show that Sonja has a purple sweater at home just like the one in the store

Ⓓ to show how hard Sonja has been trying to find a sweater like the one in the store

20 In what way are Gabrielle, Sonja, and Urie all ALIKE?

Ⓕ They like the same color.

Ⓖ They enjoy going shopping.

Ⓗ They do extra chores to earn money.

Ⓘ They save their money to buy new clothes.

21 What is Sonja's MAIN problem in the story?

Ⓐ Her friends don't like the sweater she likes.

Ⓑ She doesn't have enough money to buy something.

Ⓒ Her friends want to leave her to go to the food court.

Ⓓ She doesn't know which color would look best on her.

22 Read these sentences from the story.

But the store only had one dress in her size, and it had a large smear of dirt on the collar. When Sonja's mother brought the soiled dress to the salesclerk's attention, he had given her a discount.

Which words from the story BEST help the reader figure out what the word *soiled* means in the sentence above?

Ⓕ one dress in her size

Ⓖ a large smear of dirt

Ⓗ salesclerk's attention

Ⓘ given her a discount

23 What is the MAIN lesson that Sonja learns?

Ⓐ Buying new clothes is expensive.

Ⓑ Shopping with friends is a lot of fun.

Ⓒ Having friends who look out for you is important.

Ⓓ Making enough money to buy clothes can be difficult.

Name ______________________ Date __________

Read the article "A New Ball Game" before answering Numbers 24 through 29.

A New Ball Game

How are a peach basket and a basketball hoop alike? No, you did not misunderstand. They actually have something in common. Read the story, and you will find out!

A long time ago, there was a gym teacher named Mr. Naismith. He had a hard time keeping his class busy. His students were bored and they talked too loudly. They didn't like to stay inside in winter. Mr. Naismith tried to think of a way to keep his class busy.

Mr. Naismith had an idea. He asked someone at the school to find two boxes, but no boxes could be found. Mr. Naismith got two peach baskets and put them high above the gym floor—one basket at one end of the gym and the other basket at the other end.

Mr. Naismith had a surprise for his students the next day. When they saw the peach baskets, they laughed. Mr. Naismith told them the rules of his new game. There would be two teams. Each team would try to throw a ball into a peach basket. The teams would not play against each other. They would just try to get a ball into their own basket.

There was one main rule: when a player had the ball, he had to pass it to another player. The player who got the ball would throw it into the basket. The students had a hard time passing the ball. Everyone wanted to keep the ball and throw it in the basket.

The players could not push or hit each other. If they did, Mr. Naismith would blow his whistle and that team would get a foul. After three fouls, the other team would get a point.

Since there were no holes in the bottoms of the peach baskets, when a player threw the ball into the basket, it stayed there! Mr. Naismith had to climb a ladder to get the ball out of the basket. Then players could shoot the ball again. The game moved at a snail's pace.

Mr. Naismith thought of some changes. He cut out the bottoms of the baskets so that he wouldn't have to climb a ladder to get a ball. In order to make the game move faster, the rules of the game changed, too. The teams started to play against each other. Then players could bounce the ball.

The students loved peach basketball. They asked Mr. Naismith to play the game inside and outside, and they showed their friends how to play. Everyone raved about the game. After a while, peach baskets were changed to hoops and nets. Does this sound familiar? Peach baskets became basketball hoops. The game of basketball was invented.

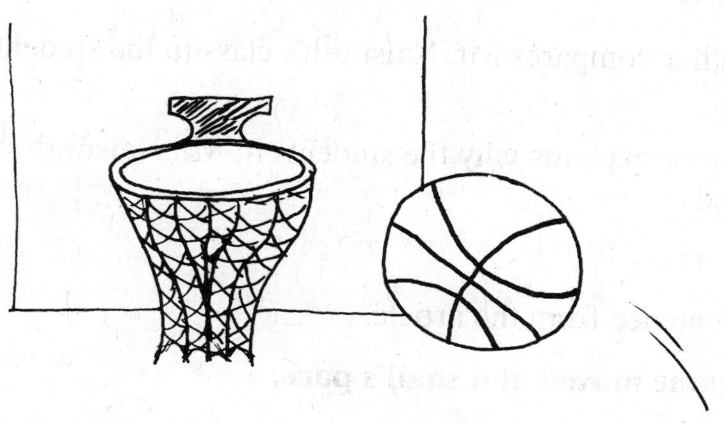

Now answer Numbers 24 through 29. Base your answers on the article "A New Ball Game."

24 Read this sentence from the story.

No, you did not misunderstand.

If *understand* means "get the idea about," then what does the word *misunderstand* mean in the sentence above?

Ⓕ to really get the idea

Ⓖ to get the wrong idea

Ⓗ to get a good idea about something

Ⓘ to be the first to get an idea about something

Name ______________________ Date ____________

25 Read this sentence from the article.

Mr. Naismith tried to think of a way to keep his class busy.

Which of the following BEST describes how the author connects this sentence to the ideas in the next paragraph?

Ⓐ The author describes the type of class that Mr. Naismith taught.

Ⓑ The author tells about an idea Mr. Naismith had to keep his class busy.

Ⓒ The author compares Mr. Naismith's class to the students' other classes.

Ⓓ The author explains why the students in Mr. Naismith's class were so bored.

26 Read this sentence from the article.

The game moved at a snail's pace.

What does the phrase *at a snail's pace* mean in the sentence above?

Ⓕ slowly

Ⓖ all at once

Ⓗ immediately

Ⓘ in a convenient way

27 What effect did Mr. Naismith's rule changes have on the game of peach basketball?

Ⓐ It made the game move faster.

Ⓑ It made the game more boring.

Ⓒ It made it harder for players to score points.

Ⓓ It made it harder for players to pass the ball.

28 Read this sentence from the article.

Everyone raved about the game.

Why does the author use the phrase *raved about* in the sentence above?

Ⓕ to show that people loved the game

Ⓖ to show that people wanted to change the game

Ⓗ to show that people knew the game's rules very well

Ⓘ to show that people played the game in different places

29 Read this sentence from the story.

Does this sound familiar?

Which word means the OPPOSITE of the word *familiar* as it is used in the sentence above?

Ⓐ easy

Ⓑ new

Ⓒ pleasant

Ⓓ tricky

Name ______________________ Date ____________

Read the story "Lazy Day" before answering Numbers 30 through 35.

Lazy Day

by Eileen Spinelli
illustrated by Stephanie Roth

One fine day, Mama woke up long after the alarm clock went off. "Today is Lazy Day!" she declared.

So breakfast was berries and bananas, and nobody cooked.

We all left our bowls in the sink and went outside where there was plenty to look at.

For the rest of the morning, we took it easy and did nothing but look.

Daddy looked at the shed that needed painting. But nobody paints on Lazy Day. So he watched the squirrels instead. They were scurrying around the yard looking for something good to eat.

Grandma looked at the weeds sprouting in her flower garden. But nobody pulls weeds on Lazy Day. So she watched the butterflies instead. They were dancing above the petunias.

Grandpa looked at his dusty red truck that needed washing. But nobody washes trucks on Lazy Day. So he watched Mrs. Albert's pet duck chase the mail carrier and got quite a giggle.

Mama watched our cat stalking a sunbeam.

I watched the sky. Two ship-shaped clouds floated by.

Lazy Day lunch was a picnic in the backyard with chunks of cheese and hunks of bread, and nobody cooked.

After lunch Mama felt like singing. So she did.

Daddy felt like smelling the roses. So he did.

Grandma felt like taking a nap.

Grandpa felt like taking off his shoes and socks.

I felt like splashing in an old garden tub. So I did.

Dinner on Lazy Day was cold leftovers on paper plates, and nobody cooked.

After dinner there was plenty to entertain us. Fireflies and moonrise. Bats against the starlight. Owls hooting. Crickets chirping. Bullfrogs croaking. Neighbors waving and joking about us lazybones lolling in rocking chairs.

Name ______________________ Date ____________

But that's how it is on Lazy Day. You don't have to do a thing. You just have to be.

Now answer Numbers 30 through 35. Base your answers on the story "Lazy Day."

30 Read this sentence from the story.

One fine day, Mama woke up long after the alarm clock went off.

What does the sentence above tell you about Mama?

Ⓕ She wakes up much later than usual.

Ⓖ She is disappointed that she overslept.

Ⓗ She enjoys waking up to an alarm clock.

Ⓘ She never wakes up at the same time every day.

31 According to the story, how are breakfast, lunch, and dinner all ALIKE?

Ⓐ All three meals are leftovers.

Ⓑ All three meals are not cooked.

Ⓒ All three meals are berries and bananas.

Ⓓ All three meals are served on paper plates.

32 Read this sentence from the article.

They were scurrying around the yard looking for something good to eat.

What does the word *scurrying* mean in the sentence above?

Ⓕ sitting

Ⓖ looking

Ⓗ making noise

Ⓘ moving quickly

33 How do the illustrations help create an overall feeling, or mood, of the story?

Ⓐ by showing how funny the characters are

Ⓑ by showing how bored the characters feel

Ⓒ by showing how relaxed the characters are

Ⓓ by showing how restless the characters feel

34 Which event takes place LAST in the story?

Ⓕ Mama sings.

Ⓖ Grandma takes a nap.

Ⓗ Daddy watches squirrels.

Ⓘ Neighbors wave and joke.

Name ________________________ Date ____________

35 What was the author's MAIN purpose for writing "Lazy Day"?

Ⓐ to tell interesting facts about holidays

Ⓑ to show people different ways to relax

Ⓒ to give information about different chores

Ⓓ to tell a story about one family's special day

Name ______________________ Date ____________

Revising and Editing

Read the introduction and the story "Telling the Truth" before answering Numbers 1 through 5.

Francisco wrote this story about an outdoor experience. Read his story and think about the changes he should make.

Telling the Truth

(1) Last spring I visited my cousins, Hilda and Hector, for a week. (2) They live in denver, Colorado. (3) The first day, they took me mountain biking. (4) I can ride a regular bike I had never ridden a mountain bike. (5) Hilda let me use her extra mountain bike and helmet. (6) I practiced riding the bike in my cousins' neighborhood. (7) It was easy—the hard part came later.

(8) We went to a forest that has biking trails through it. (9) I was enjoying the ride until we came to a steep hill. (10) My legs began to ache as I pedaled up the hill. (11) We came to a downhill part that scared me. (12) Somehow I got down the hill. (13) Without falling. (14) I wasn't enjoying mountain biking, but I didn't want to tell my cousins. (15) When the ride was over that day I was so glad. (16) I pretended I'd had a great time, though.

(17) The next day, my cousins said, "Let's ride mountain bikes again!" (18) I didn't want to say no, but I had to tell them the truth. (19) They didn't miend at all. (20) We decided to visit the aquarium

instead, where we saw an exhibit called "Marine adventures."

(21) That was a lot more fun than mountain biking!

Now answer Numbers 1 through 5. Base your answers on the changes Francisco should make.

1. What is the BEST way to revise sentence 4?

   Ⓐ I can ride a regular bike, I had never ridden a mountain bike.

   Ⓑ I can ride a regular bike so I had never ridden a mountain bike.

   Ⓒ I can ride a regular bike, but I had never ridden a mountain bike.

   Ⓓ I can ride a regular bike, then I had never ridden a mountain bike.

2. What is the BEST way to rewrite sentence 11?

   Ⓕ We came to a downhill. Part that scared me.

   Ⓖ First, we came to a downhill part that scared me.

   Ⓗ Next, we came to a downhill part that scared me.

   Ⓘ Today, we came to a downhill part that scared me.

3. What is the BEST way to revise sentences 12 and 13?

   Ⓐ Somehow I got down the hill without falling.

   Ⓑ Somehow I got down the hill; without falling.

   Ⓒ Without falling. Somehow I got down the hill.

   Ⓓ Somehow I got, down the hill without falling.

4. What change should be made in sentence 19?

   Ⓕ change ***They*** to **Them**

   Ⓖ change ***didn't*** to **did'nt**

   Ⓗ change ***miend*** to **mind**

   Ⓘ change ***at all*** to **atall**

5. What change should be made in sentence 20?

   Ⓐ change ***decided*** to **decide**

   Ⓑ change ***the*** to **a**

   Ⓒ change ***Marine*** to **marine**

   Ⓓ change ***adventures*** to **Adventures**

Name ________________________ Date ______________

Read the introduction and the article "We All Need Sleep" before answering Numbers 6 through 10.

Hailey wrote this article about sleep. Read her article and think about the changes she should make.

We All Need Sleep

(1) A good night's sleep is important to our health and learning. (2) Have you noticed how you feel when you don't get enough sleep? (3) Growing kids need about ten hours of sleep each night.

(4) Animals also need sleep. (5) Octopuses, otters, foxs, and fruit flies all snooze and slumber. (6) Researchers are learning about the sleep patterns of different animals. (7) Some animals seam to need more sleep than others. (8) For example, an elephant only sleeps for two to four hours a day, but an opossum

sleeps for almast twenty hours a day. (9) Some animals, such as horses, sleep standing up. (10) Others, such as bats, upside down.

(11) Some animals are half-awake when they are sleeping. (12) Whales and dolphins keep one eye open and half of their brains awake when they sleep to protect themselves in the Ocean. (13) When ducks sleep in a group, the birds on the outside edge sleep with half their brains awake and their eyes partially open.

(14) Scientists still have a lot to learn about sleep in people and in animals. (15) They know one thing for sure, though. (16) Whether you're a person or a porcupine, you can't live without sleep.

Now answer Numbers 6 through 10. Base your answers on the changes Hailey should make.

6 What change should be made in sentence 5?

- Ⓕ change ***octopuses*** to **octopuss**
- Ⓖ change ***foxs*** to **foxes**
- Ⓗ add a period after ***snooze***
- Ⓘ change the period to a question mark

Name ______________________ Date ____________

7 What change should be made in sentence 7?

Ⓐ change ***animals*** to **animales**

Ⓑ change ***seam*** to **seem**

Ⓒ change ***than*** to **and**

Ⓓ change the period to a question mark

8 What change should be made in sentence 8?

Ⓕ change ***elephant*** to **elephants**

Ⓖ change ***two*** to **too**

Ⓗ change ***almast*** to **almost**

Ⓘ change ***hours*** to **hour**

9 What is the BEST way to revise sentence 10?

Ⓐ Others such as bats upside down.

Ⓑ Others, such as bats upside down.

Ⓒ Others, such as bats, upside down?

Ⓓ Others, such as bats, sleep upside down.

10 What change should be made in sentence 12?

Ⓕ change ***Whales*** to **Whals**

Ⓖ change ***dolphins*** to **Dolphins**

Ⓗ insert a period after ***open***

Ⓘ change ***Ocean*** to **ocean**

Name ____________________ Date __________

Writing to Narrate

Read the prompt and plan your response.

> **Most people have a good memory of a time they did something fun.**
>
> **Think about a time you did something fun.**
>
> **Now write a story about the time you did something fun.**

Planning Page

Use this space to make your notes before you begin writing. The writing on this page will NOT be scored.

Name ______________________ Date ____________

Begin writing your response here. The writing on this page and the next page WILL be scored.

Name ______________________ Date ____________

Name ____________________ Date __________

Reading Complex Text

Read the story "An Unexpected Lesson." As you read, stop and answer each question. Use evidence from the story to support your answers.

An Unexpected Lesson

I remember seeing Miss Togut in the hallways. Her third-grade students were lined up behind her. They formed two lines in order of height, one for the girls and one for the boys. I was in the second grade and had to stand in line with my own class, but not like that.

"Stay in a straight line, girls, right behind the person in front of you," Miss Togut boomed. "Look straight ahead, boys, not to the side and keep your hands to yourself." Her voice was so loud you could easily mistake it for one of the overhead loudspeakers in the hallways. It seemed to make the walls vibrate.

Miss Togut had what was called a beehive hairdo. It was the color of gold spray paint and swirled upward. I could imagine real bees swarming around her head, and I wanted to get about as close to her as I did to them. She wore black cat-eye glasses. Those glasses made her look like a hungry cat ready to pounce! When I didn't see her coming, her voice alone made my hair stand on end. Each time that happened, one thought would cross my mind. "Please, don't be my teacher next year."

When the envelopes were passed out at the end of second grade, I tore mine open. There it was: my third-grade teacher would be Miss Togut. I decided right away I was in for a long and difficult year ahead.

1. What does the narrator think about Miss Togut? What details in the story show this?

____

____

____

Name ______________________ Date ______________

At the start of third grade, I walked into Miss Togut's classroom trembling with fear. I was prepared for the worst and held my breath to see what would happen. Miss Togut took attendance. Sitting stick straight in a chair at her desk, she looked carefully at each student as she read the names. She wasn't inspecting us though. It soon became clear that she wanted to get to know us.

"Lisa Blau," she read, then looked around the room and waited till a dark-haired girl wearing a plaid jumper quietly raised her hand. "Jonathan Guerra, Victor Cha," she read. Each time she waited to see the owner of each name. She then asked a simple question. What games do you like to play on a rainy day? What is your favorite fall color? Tell me, how is your older brother, Jonathan?

As she went down the list, I was surprised at the way her voice was so unlike the voice I had heard before. It was softer and kinder. It was as if she knew the students would be a little worried that first day of school and she wanted them to know that was okay. More surprising than the change in her voice, was the change in her face. When I would see her in the hallway, her bright red lipstick made a thin straight line across her face. Now, it was as if a crack in a thick wall was letting the light into a dark room. She was not going to pounce after all.

Name ______________________ Date ____________

2 How do the narrator's feelings about Miss Togut change?

____

____

____

As the days and weeks passed, the surprises kept coming. Miss Togut knew how to tell stories. She especially knew how to use her voice. She could lower it to hold us in suspense or raise it to act out a commanding character. With Miss Togut even math became suspenseful. It turned into a puzzle that you couldn't help wanting to solve.

Name ____________________ Date ______________

3 What do the photographs tell about the narrator's experience?

____

____

____

Yet nothing was ever quite as much of a puzzle to me as how the Miss Togut I knew in the hallway could be the same one I knew now. How could she be so different? How could I have been so wrong?

This was school, but the lessons I was learning were not only the ones my teacher was trying to teach. And maybe, just maybe, Miss Togut knew just what she was doing. After all, walking 32 third-graders down a crowded hallway isn't always a walk in the park.

4 FIRST tell what lesson the narrator learns from Miss Togut. Then explain how Miss Togut teaches this lesson to the narrator.

____

____

____

____

____

Name ______________________ Date ______________

Reading and Analyzing Text

Read the story "Treasures Found" before answering Numbers 1 through 18.

Treasures Found

Katie was strolling down the main hall at school. The bell had just rung and signaled the end of another school week. Katie's friend Xavier walked alongside her, telling her about his plans for the weekend. Suddenly Katie stopped listening as a sign on the wall caught her eye. It shouted "ART CONTEST" in large, bold letters across the top. Katie read aloud the information on the sign.

Students in all grades can enter the art contest. Pick up an entry form in the school office, fill it in, and return it to the office by February 6. All artwork is due by March 1. Famous wood carver Antonio Gonzalez will be one of the judges. Contest winners will be announced on March 5.

Katie turned to Xavier and said excitedly, "I'm going to submit something to the contest!" As Katie got on the bus, her head buzzed with ideas. She thought about painting a picture of her dog, Biscuit. Then she thought about making something with clay. There were so many possible choices!

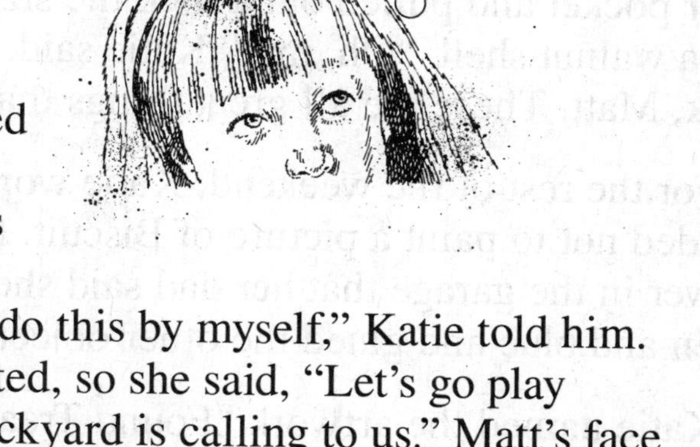

When she got home, Katie continued to imagine ideas for her artwork. She made a few sketches of Biscuit. Katie's younger brother wanted to help her with the artwork. "No, Matt, I have to do this by myself," Katie told him. She could see that Matt was disappointed, so she said, "Let's go play outside! It's a beautiful day, and the backyard is calling to us." Matt's face brightened as he ran ahead of her out the door.

After playing for some time, the two stopped to wander through their backyard. "Look!" said Matt, "I found a pretty feather!" He picked up the blue feather and showed it to Katie. Then he put it in his pocket and continued to look on the lawn. “I found something else,” he called as he ran over to Katie and handed her three white pebbles.

Katie was finding interesting things, too. She found some thin, curly twigs and crisp brown leaves. Katie began to picture a design made from the objects they had found. She asked Matt to help her collect more items. After some intense searching, they went back inside.

Katie put a sheet of poster board on the kitchen table. Then she and Matt spread out the objects they had found on it. “Watch this,” Katie told Matt. She began to arrange the objects, putting items with different textures together. She put the smooth white pebbles next to the crunchy brown leaves. She sprinkled dried grass here and there on the board. Katie studied the arrangement and said, “It needs a few more things.”

Matt leapt from his chair and declared, “I’ll find some more!” He hurried out the back door again. Katie watched as her brother sat on the grass and inspected the ground carefully. Then he moved to another place in the yard. Katie returned to arranging the objects. About thirty minutes later, Matt came back inside. His pockets bulged with the treasures he’d found in the yard.

“Let’s see what you’ve found,” Katie said. Matt dug into one pocket and produced two old pennies and a snail shell. He reached into the other pocket and pulled out a rock the size of his fist, a snack wrapper, and a walnut shell. “Oh, my!” Katie said. “I really appreciate your hard work, Matt. These are all great things that can be used in the artwork.”

For the rest of the weekend, Katie worked on her project. She had decided not to paint a picture of Biscuit. Instead, she found an old drawer in the garage that her dad said she could have. Katie painted it green and blue and glued the other objects to its inside.

Katie named the artwork “Found Treasures” and entered it in the contest. She did not win the art contest, but she was only a little disappointed. The judges announced that she had won “honorable mention.” This meant that her artwork was good enough to be recognized as special. Katie felt proud when the judges gave her a ribbon and lots of applause. Katie knew that Matt would be excited about the ribbon. She could hardly wait to get home that day to give it to him.

Now answer Numbers 1 through 18. Base your answers on the story "Treasures Found."

1. At the beginning of the story, why does Katie stop listening to Xavier?

   Ⓐ She is late for the school bus.

   Ⓑ She is bored by what Xavier says.

   Ⓒ She is thinking about her artwork.

   Ⓓ She sees the sign for the art contest.

2. Read this sentence from the story.

   It shouted "ART CONTEST" in large, bold letters across the top.

   Why does the author compare the sign to someone shouting in the sentence above?

   Ⓕ to show that Katie nearly missed the sign

   Ⓖ to show that the sign got Katie's attention

   Ⓗ to show that the sign contains lots of information

   Ⓘ to show that Xavier didn't want Katie to see the sign

Name ______________________ Date ______________

3 Read this sentence from the story.

Contest winners will be ann<u>ou</u>nced on March 5.

Which word has the same sound as the underlined part of the word *announced*?

Ⓐ brown

Ⓑ could

Ⓒ smooth

Ⓓ through

4 Read this sentence from the story.

There were so many possible choices!

What does the word *possible* mean in the sentence above?

Ⓕ done again

Ⓖ able to be done

Ⓗ done in the past

Ⓘ done in a slow way

5 Read this sentence from the story.

When she got home, Katie continued to imagine ideas for her artwork.

What does the word *imagine* mean in the sentence above?

Ⓐ set aside

Ⓑ put on display

Ⓒ start from the beginning

Ⓓ form a mental picture of

Name _______________________ Date ___________

6 Read this sentence from the story.

She made a few sketches of Biscuit.

What does the word *sketches* mean in the sentence above?

Ⓕ paintings

Ⓖ written accounts

Ⓗ rough drawings or outlines

Ⓘ small models, often made of clay

7 Which of the following can the reader BEST tell from the story?

Ⓐ Katie is a good student.

Ⓑ Xavier lives near Katie.

Ⓒ Katie enjoys making art.

Ⓓ Matt does not like to go outside.

8 What does the illustration show readers about Katie?

Ⓕ She has not seen the sign for the art contest.

Ⓖ She has decided what to create for her artwork.

Ⓗ She is playing in the backyard with her brother.

Ⓘ She is considering different ideas for her artwork.

Name ________________________ Date ______________

9 Read these sentences from the story.

She could see that Matt was disappointed, so she said, "Let's go play outside! It's a beautiful day, and the backyard is calling to us."

What does the author compare the backyard to in the sentence above?

Ⓐ a person who is beautiful

Ⓑ a person who has just awakened

Ⓒ a person inviting others to join him or her

Ⓓ a person feeling sorry for himself or herself

10 Read this sentence from the story.

Then he put it in his pocket and continued to look on the <u>law</u>n.

Which word has the same sound as the underlined part of the word *lawn*?

Ⓕ cross

Ⓖ down

Ⓗ latch

Ⓘ nail

11 Why does Katie decide NOT to paint a picture of Biscuit?

Ⓐ She is not pleased with her painting.

Ⓑ Biscuit will not sit still for a painting.

Ⓒ She discovers another way to make artwork.

Ⓓ Matt asks her to use found objects to make artwork.

12 Read this sentence from the story.

Matt leapt from his chair and declared, "I'll find some more!"

Why does the author use the word *leapt* instead of *got up*?

Ⓕ to show that Matt is excited

Ⓖ to show that the chair is unsteady

Ⓗ to show that Matt does not want to help Katie

Ⓘ to show that Matt got out of his chair carefully

13 Read this sentence from the story.

Katie returned to arranging the objects.

Which of these shows the correct way to divide the word *returned* into syllables?

Ⓐ retur • ned

Ⓑ re • turned

Ⓒ r • eturned

Ⓓ ret • urned

14 Read this sentence from the story.

His pockets bulged with the treasures he'd found in the yard.

Which word means almost the SAME as the word *bulged* in the sentence above?

Ⓕ closed

Ⓖ fell

Ⓗ shrunk

Ⓘ swelled

Name ____________________ Date __________

15 How does Matt MOST LIKELY feel when Katie uses his objects in her artwork?

Ⓐ angry

Ⓑ pleased

Ⓒ sad

Ⓓ unlucky

16 Read this sentence from the story.

He reached into the other pocket and pulled out a rock the size of his fist, a snack <u>wr</u>apper, and a walnut shell.

Which word has the same sound as the underlined part of the word *wrapper*?

Ⓕ light

Ⓖ ring

Ⓗ well

Ⓘ when

Name ____________________ Date ____________

17 Read the dictionary entry below.

ap•pre•ci•ate \ə-prē'shē-āt'\ *verb* **1.** to be grateful. **2.** to understand. **3.** to recognize. **4.** to grown in number.

Read this sentence from the story.

"I really appreciate your hard work, Matt."

Which meaning BEST fits the way the word *appreciate* is used in the sentence above?

Ⓐ meaning 1

Ⓑ meaning 2

Ⓒ meaning 3

Ⓓ meaning 4

18 Read this sentence from the story.

Katie felt proud when the judges gave her a ribbon and lots of applause.

What does the word *applause* mean in the sentence above?

Ⓕ words of praise

Ⓖ clapping to show approval

Ⓗ objects arranged in a particular pattern

Ⓘ works of art made out of various materials

Name ______________________ Date ______________

Read the brochure "Pine Elementary School Science Fair" before answering Numbers 19 through 35.

Pine Elementary School Science Fair

PINE ELEMENTARY SCHOOL PRESENTS

Student Science Fair

For Students in Grades K–5

Dates: October 30–31

Location: Pine Elementary School Gym

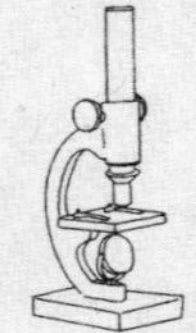

Explore Your World . . . Think Like a Scientist

The Student Science Fair offers a great way for you to put your science knowledge to use! Whether or not you win, you'll have fun at this contest.

Science Fair Events

There is plenty to do during the science fair. Of course, you'll want to take a look at all of the students' projects. There will be other exciting things to see and do as well. These events will highlight the wonderful world of science. The big event is the announcement of the winners in each grade. This announcement will take place at the awards ceremony on Friday afternoon. Many of the other events are listed below.

Name ______________________ Date ______________

Meet a Robot!

Can people and robots work together? Learn about the latest research being done to make that happen. Scientists will be at the fair on Thursday, October 30, with Modo. What's Modo? It is a robot helper being developed to help people with jobs they do. Learn how Modo's large blue eyes are able to "see." Watch Modo grasp objects and wiggle them to get a feel for their size. Then see how Modo places the objects on a shelf. Touch Modo on the arm. Watch what happens! It will respond to your touch. If you push it too hard, it will say, "Ouch!"

Modo's visit is a rare public appearance, since the robot does not often leave the laboratory. Be sure to see this amazing robot while you have the chance!

More Robots!

The fair will also have other types of robots. They will range from simple ones to more complicated machines. Scientists who built the robots will be at the science fair to show what their inventions can do. They will explain how a robot is "born." The scientists will also answer questions about the design and building of the robots.

Our Own Thomas Edison

Make sure you're in the gym at 10:00 A.M. on Friday. That's when local genius Ray Allen will give a talk about his life as an inventor. He will also show some of his early gadgets. At the end of his talk, Mr. Allen will take questions from the audience.

SCIENCE FAIR SCHEDULE

Registration
October 27 7:30 A.M.–5:00 P.M.

Set-up of Projects
October 28 10:00 A.M.–3:00 P.M.
October 29 10:00 A.M.–3:00 P.M.

Science Fair Viewing
October 30 10:00 A.M.–3:00 P.M.
October 31 10:00 A.M.–3:00 P.M.

Awards Presentation
October 31 1:00 P.M.

Name ______________________ Date ______________

HOW TO SIGN UP

Get a sign-up form in the Pine Elementary School office. Complete the form and turn it in by 5:00 P.M. on Monday, October 27. You will also receive a science fair booklet. The booklet will give you suggestions on how to choose a topic for a science fair project and how to create a display. It will also list sources of ideas for projects. Information on what you must include in a display can be found in the booklet.

WHY TAKE PART IN THE SCIENCE FAIR?

You can

- explore the world of science in a project of your choice.
- share your knowledge and interests with others.
- meet scientists and get their valuable advice.

This is last year's winner!

- view your classmates' thrilling science projects.
- see who wins the science prize.

WHO ARE THE JUDGES?

The Pine Elementary School Science Committee will choose the judges, which will include science teachers and local scientists.

Contact Information

If you have any questions, contact Jenny McAllister at 555-1845 or Wynn Adams at 555-2331.

Now answer Numbers 19 through 35. Base your answers on the brochure "Pine Elementary School Science Fair."

19 What is the main idea of this brochure?

Ⓐ a school science fair

Ⓑ a public appearance

Ⓒ an awards ceremony

Ⓓ a schedule of events

20 Read this sentence from the brochure.

This announcement will take place at the awards ceremony on Friday afternoon.

Which word means almost the SAME as the word *awards*, as used in the sentence above?

Ⓕ activities

Ⓖ prizes

Ⓗ projects

Ⓘ winners

21 Read this sentence from the brochure.

Learn ab<u>ou</u>t the latest research being done to make that happen.

Which word has the same sound as the underlined part of the word *about*?

Ⓐ crowd

Ⓑ look

Ⓒ show

Ⓓ world

Name ______________________ Date ______________

22 Read this sentence from the brochure.

Learn about the latest research being done to make that happen.

What does the word *research* mean in the sentence above?

Ⓕ fact finding

Ⓖ using machines

Ⓗ working with others

Ⓘ putting parts together

23 What can the reader tell from the information in the paragraph *Meet a Robot!*?

Ⓐ Modo falls over easily.

Ⓑ Ray Allen invented Modo.

Ⓒ Modo robots will be for sale.

Ⓓ Scientists are still developing Modo.

24 Read this sentence from the brochure.

Watch Modo grasp objects and wiggle them to get a feel for their size.

What does the word *grasp* mean as used in the sentence above?

Ⓕ remove

Ⓖ glance at

Ⓗ search for

Ⓘ hold tightly

Name ______________________ Date ____________

25 Read this sentence from the brochure.

Modo's visit is a rare public appearance, since the robot does not often leave the laboratory.

What does the word *laboratory* mean in the sentence above?

Ⓐ the place where a scientist lives

Ⓑ the place where a scientists works

Ⓒ a place where a science fair is held

Ⓓ a place where students learn about science

26 Read this sentence from the brochure.

They will range from simple ones to more complicated machines.

What does the word *complicated* mean in the sentence above?

Ⓕ complex

Ⓖ decorated

Ⓗ plain

Ⓘ shiny

27 Read this sentence from the brochure.

That's when local genius Ray Allen will give a talk about his life as an inventor.

What does the word *genius* mean in the sentence above?

Ⓐ a type of scientist

Ⓑ a very smart person

Ⓒ a person who is famous

Ⓓ a person who gives speeches

Name ______________________ Date ______________

28 Why will many students be in the gym at 1:00 P.M. on October 31?

Ⓕ Modo will appear.

Ⓖ Registration takes place.

Ⓗ The awards will be announced.

Ⓘ Ray Allen will give an interview.

29 Read this sentence from the brochure.

At the end of his talk, Mr. Allen will take questions from the audience.

Which word has the same sound as the underlined part of the word *audience*?

Ⓐ class

Ⓑ range

Ⓒ share

Ⓓ walk

30 Where can students get sign-up forms for the science fair?

Ⓕ in the gym

Ⓖ in the office

Ⓗ in the library

Ⓘ in the cafeteria

Name ________________________ Date ______________

31 Read these words from the brochure.

- **meet scientists and get their valuable advice.**

If the word *value* means "worth" or "use," what does the word *valuable* mean?

Ⓐ of little worth or use
Ⓑ worthwhile or useful
Ⓒ without worth or use
Ⓓ of unknown worth or use

32 According to the information in the section *WHY TAKE PART IN THE SCIENCE FAIR?,* what can students who take part in the fair do?

Ⓕ design a robot
Ⓖ meet scientists
Ⓗ judge a contest
Ⓘ become scientists

33 What can readers learn about the science fair by looking at the pictures in the brochure?

Ⓐ Most schools have science fairs.
Ⓑ There will be a robot at the science fair.
Ⓒ A famous scientist will be at the science fair.
Ⓓ Students should build a robot for the science fair.

34 In what way do the headings in dark type help the reader?

Ⓕ They help the reader understand the pictures in the brochure.
Ⓖ They help the reader learn important dates in the science fair.
Ⓗ They help the reader find important information about the fair.
Ⓘ They help the reader find phone numbers for contact information.

Name ______________________ Date ____________

35 Read these words from the brochure.

- **view your classmates' thrilling science projects.**

Which word means almost the SAME as the word *thrilling*?

Ⓐ exciting

Ⓑ expecting

Ⓒ winning

Ⓓ working

Name ______________________ Date ____________

Revising and Editing

Read the introduction and the story "Birthday Chickens" before answering Numbers 1 through 5.

Elliot wrote this story about a special gift that he received. Read his story and think about the changes he should make.

Birthday Chickens

(1) Some people receive toys and games for their birthdays, while others receive decorated cards. (2) Last year, I got chickens for this special day. (3) That was the most thoughtful present ever, because I have wanted to raise chickens ever since my family and I moved to the country. (4) Our neighbor has plenty of livestock, including chickens, and our neighbor would let me help collect eggs. (5) I enjoyed watching the rooster and hens scratch around in her yard, pecking the ground for food. (6) I know it sounds silly, but I just loved those chickens and wanted some of my very own.

(7) First, I went to the library and checked out books about chickens. (8) Next, I asked Mom and Dad to let me raise chickens. (9) I told them that I had read everything I could find about raising and taking care of chickens. (10) "We just want to make sure you are really going to look after them" Mom said. (11) I promised that the chickens would become my responsibility and reminded them that we would also have free eggs! (12) Then Mom, Dad, and I built

a coop next to our barn. (13) We also built a fence around the coop (14) This let the chickens have a place to roam and peck. (15) It would also keep them safe from other animals.

(16) On my birthday, I came home from school, not expecting anything special. (17) Guess what was in the coop? (18) There were four beautiful and fluffy little baby chicks! (19) That's much better than a toy or a game. (20) A toy or a game is not as good.

Now answer Numbers 1 through 5. Base your answers on the changes Elliot should make.

1. What is the BEST way to revise sentence 4?

   Ⓐ Our neighbor has plenty of livestock, including chickens, and she would let me help collect eggs.

   Ⓑ Our neighbor has plenty of livestock, including chickens. Our neighbor would let me help collect eggs.

   Ⓒ Our neighbor have plenty of livestock, including chickens, and our neighbor would let me help collect eggs.

   Ⓓ Our neighbor she has livestock and chickens, and our neighbor would let me help collect eggs.

2. Which sentence could BEST be added before sentence 7?

   Ⓕ I wanted my own chickens more than anything else.

   Ⓖ My neighbor has several chickens.

   Ⓗ I prepared a plan that was guaranteed to work.

   Ⓘ I asked Mom and Dad if I could have chickens.

Name ____________________ Date __________

3. What revision should be made in sentence 10?

Ⓐ "We just want to make sure you are really going to look after them said Mom."

Ⓑ "We just want to make sure you are really going to look after them, said Mom."

Ⓒ "We just want to make sure you are really going to look after them," said Mom.

Ⓓ "We just want to make sure you are really going to look after them," said Mom."

4. Which word in sentence 11 is an abstract noun?

Ⓕ chickens

Ⓖ responsibility

Ⓗ them

Ⓘ eggs

5. Which sentence does NOT belong in this story?

Ⓐ sentence 3

Ⓑ sentence 5

Ⓒ sentence 11

Ⓓ sentence 20

Name ______________________ Date ____________

Read the introduction and the article "Our National Bird" before answering Numbers 6 through 10.

Tanya wrote this article about the bald eagle. Read her article and think about the changes she should make.

Our National Bird

(1) Can you name the national bird of the United States? (2) It's the bald eagle. (3) Of course, the bald eagle's rownd head is not really bald. (4) Its name comes from the Old English word balde, which means "white." (5) Both the heads and tails of bald eagles are white.

(6) Female bald eagles are typically larger than male bald eagles. (7) The wings of a female bald eagle stretched about 8 feet from wing tip to wing tip. (8) That length is about the distance from the floor to the ceiling of most rooms!

Name ____________________ Date ____________

(9) Bald eagles' nests are larger than any other bird in North America. (10) Female bald eagles builds their nests at the top of tall trees in order to protect their eggs. (11) Baby eagles are light gray when they are born. (12) Later, they turn brown and white.

(13) In fact, they can fly to heights of up to 10,000 feet. (14) They swoop down from above and animals such as fish. (15) An eagle glides over the water, grabs a fish with its feet, and flies away to eat it.

(16) Bald eagles can live for 30 years or more. (17) They were once almost extinct, or completely destroyed, because of pollution and hunting. (18) Bald eagles are no longer in danger of extinction because of laws passed to protect bald eagles.

Now answer Numbers 6 through 10. Base your answers on the changes Tanya should make.

6. What change should be made in sentence 3?
   - Ⓕ change the comma to a period
   - Ⓖ change ***bald*** to **bold**
   - Ⓗ change ***rownd*** to **round**
   - Ⓘ change ***really*** to **realy**

Name ______________________ Date __________

7 What change should be made in sentence 7?

Ⓐ change ***female*** to **females**

Ⓑ change ***stretched*** to **stretch**

Ⓒ change ***feet*** to **foot**

Ⓓ add a comma after ***from***

8 What change should be made in sentence 10?

Ⓕ change ***builds*** to **build**

Ⓖ add a comma after ***top***

Ⓗ change ***to*** to **too**

Ⓘ change the period to a question mark

9 Which sentence could BEST be added before sentence 13?

Ⓐ Bald eagles are proud birds.

Ⓑ Bald eagles have white heads.

Ⓒ Bald eagles are masters of the sky.

Ⓓ Bald eagles are no longer in danger.

10 What is the BEST way to revise sentence 18?

Ⓕ Bald eagles are no longer in danger, laws passed to protect them from extinction.

Ⓖ Bald eagles are no longer in danger of extinction because of laws passed to protect them.

Ⓗ Bald eagles are no longer in danger because of the laws of extinction passed to protect bald eagles.

Ⓘ Because of laws passed to protect bald eagles are no longer in danger of extinction because of them.

Name ____________________________ Date ______________

Writing Opinions

Read the story "A Visit with Aunt Liza" before responding to the prompt.

A Visit with Aunt Liza

As Andy sat on a rock near the park entrance, he stared at the group of people gathered around his Aunt Liza. It was the first time that Andy had seen his Aunt Liza at work as a park ranger.

"That's the end of the tour," Aunt Liza told the group of park visitors. "I hope you enjoyed learning about the park and its animals."

The crowd clapped and thanked Aunt Liza for sharing so much information about the park and its history. Aunt Liza answered a few more questions and then walked over to Andy. "Are you ready for your personal tour of the park?" Aunt Liza asked him.

Andy slowly nodded his head and looked around him carefully. He had been excited about this visit with his aunt, but he was anxious about the possible dangers in the woods. Andy lived in the city where he was used to seeing animals like squirrels and raccoons, not snakes and bears.

"Stand up," Aunt Liza encouraged, "and let's get going."

Andy got up and started walking next to Aunt Liza. Heading down the trail and glancing at his feet, Andy asked, "What about the snakes?"

"We won't bother the snakes," answered Aunt Liza, patting Andy on the back to try and comfort him.

"You can count on that," Andy muttered. He felt like a fish out of water as he jumped at the sound of leaves crackling under his feet. Andy missed the city's busy sidewalks and familiar smells, and he missed the clean, shiny floors in the apartment building where his family lived.

Aunt Liza pointed at something in a tree down the trail as a blue wing flashed and swooped away.

"Mountain bluebird . . . " Aunt Liza noted as her voice trailed off.

Andy looked at his aunt and noticed she stood speechless and frozen in place.

Name ______________________________ Date ______________

"What's wrong?" Andy asked as he followed the direction of Aunt Liza's stare. Then he saw it—a bear, and it was looking at them.

Aunt Liza said softly, "It's okay, Andy. This bear seems to sense that we aren't a danger to her. Let's slowly walk back the way we came."

Andy was shaking like a leaf as he began walking backwards up the trail, but he was relieved to see that the bear did not follow them. Back at the park entrance, Andy asked Aunt Liza, "Were you scared?"

"Yes, I was," answered Aunt Liza.

"Why do you like the mountains when there are bears, snakes, and other animals that can hurt you?" asked Andy.

Aunt Liza said, "The mountains are my home. I'm a part of this area, the same as the bears and snakes."

"The same way that I'm a part of the city," Andy said.

Aunt Liza nodded and smiled, "Just like that, Andy."

"I think I'll stay in the city," Andy said with a nervous laugh.

Changing the subject, Aunt Liza smiled as she said, "I'm as hungry as a bear. Why don't we go get something to eat?"

Name ______________________ Date ____________

Now respond to the prompt. Base your response on the story "A Visit with Aunt Liza."

> **In "A Visit with Aunt Liza," Andy says that he is "a part of the city."**
>
> **Think about whether or not he should change his mind about NOT liking mountain areas.**
>
> **Write a response that tells why or why not.**

Planning Page

Use this space to make your notes before you begin writing. The writing on this page will NOT be scored.

Name ______________________ Date ____________

Begin writing your response here. The writing on this page and the next page WILL be scored.

Name ______________________ Date ____________

Name ______________________ Date ____________

Reading Complex Text

Read the legends "How Winter Came to Be" and "How the Sun Came into the World." As you read, stop and answer each question. Use evidence from the legends to support your answers.

How Winter Came to Be:

A Zuni Legend

Long ago, it was always summer, and it was always dark.

The Sun and the Moon lived somewhere on earth, not in the sky. For this reason, it was always warm, but there was no light in the sky.

Coyote was trying to hunt and find food, but he was not having much success. He had trouble seeing in the dark. Coyote knew Eagle was an excellent hunter. He thought that Eagle might be able to help him.

1. Why is Coyote having trouble finding food?

____

____

____

"Eagle!" Coyote called up to Eagle in the sky. "Come hunt with me. Surely we can catch more together than we can apart."

"You might be right, Coyote," Eagle said. "Let us try it."

The two began hunting. Eagle had much success, but Coyote could find nothing but some bugs.

"Coyote, what is wrong?" asked Eagle.

"It is too dark for me to see," said Coyote.

Name ______________________ Date ______________

Eagle thought for a moment and said, "I know of some people called the Kachinas. They have the Sun and the Moon in a box. Let us go there."

Eagle and Coyote walked for a long time. Eventually they came to the land of the Kachinas. The Kachinas invited Eagle and Coyote to sit with them and share a meal. Later, when everyone had gone to sleep, Eagle grabbed the box that kept the Sun and the Moon. Then he and Coyote ran away.

After they had run for a long time, Coyote began to bother Eagle.

"Please, Eagle," Coyote pleaded, "let me carry the box."

"No, Coyote," said Eagle sternly, "I do not trust you with the box."

Eventually, however, Eagle got tired of Coyote's whining. "Fine, Coyote, take the box, but do not open it."

So Coyote carried the box for some time, but soon his curiosity got the better of him. I must just peek inside the box, he thought to himself.

Coyote opened the box and the Sun and the Moon escaped. They flew up into the sky, far away from Eagle, Coyote, and the land, taking their warmth with them. Now the Sun and the Moon live in the sky. Summer only comes when they move close to the earth. Otherwise, it is winter.

2. What does this legend try to explain?

____

____

____

How the Sun Came into the World:
A Haida Legend

The world was once a very dark place. Raven was irritated by the constant darkness. He was constantly bumping into things and having to feel his way around.

One day Raven heard about an old man who lived alone with his daughter. He learned that the old man kept a box in his house. The box contained the Sun. Raven decided he would steal the Sun so it could light the world. Soon Raven had come up with a plan.

One day, the old man's daughter left the house to gather water from the river. Raven heard her coming and quickly changed himself into a human baby. The daughter found the human baby and instantly fell in love with it. She brought it back to her father.

The old man thought the baby had an odd look, but he agreed they could keep it. Both the old man and his daughter loved the baby until it grew into a small boy.

One day the boy pointed at the small box that held the Sun. "What's in there?" asked the boy.

The old man growled like a bear. "Do not worry about it. And never touch that box."

3. What do the words *growled like a bear* tell the reader about the old man?

____

____

____

Name ______________________ Date ______________

The boy was silent, but a short while later he was asking about the box again. The old man tried to ignore him, but he eventually gave in to the boy.

"Okay, okay, I will show you," said the old man. He opened the box and pulled out the Sun. "Catch!" said the old man as he threw the Sun to the boy.

The boy, who was Raven, laughed like a child. He tossed the Sun back to the old man. Soon they were playing a game, tossing the Sun back and forth. The old man laughed at this fun, too.

Then, as the old man tossed the Sun to the boy, the boy suddenly turned himself back into Raven. He caught the ball in his beak, and he flew up threw a hole in the roof of the house.

This is how the Sun came to light the world.

4 Explain one way in which Coyote and Raven are SIMILAR. Then explain one way in which they are DIFFERENT.

____

____

____

____

____

Name ____________________ Date __________

Reading and Analyzing Text

Read the story "The Talking Yam: An African Folktale" before answering Numbers 1 through 6.

An African Folktale

retold by Marilyn Helmer
illustrated by Josée Masse

One day, a farmer decided to dig up some yams to sell at the marketplace. As he worked, he sang:

Sweet, sweet yam, so fine,

Sweet, sweet yam, all mine!

He had just pulled the first yam from the earth when it called out to him. "All yours? What are you talking about? Where were you when it was time to weed me and water me?"

The farmer was so scared that he jumped to his feet and raced off down the road. By the river, he passed a fisherman with a large fish in his net.

"Why are you running so hard on such a hot day?" asked the fisherman.

"My yam talked to me!" said the frightened farmer.

The fisherman rolled his eyes. "I've never heard of anything so ridiculous," he said.

"I agree," said the fish. "Everyone knows that yams can't talk."

Name ______________________ Date ______________

The fisherman was so surprised that he threw the fish back into the river. Then he scrambled to his feet and ran on down the road, right on the farmer's heels.

As the farmer and the fisherman rounded a bend, they came upon a girl carrying a large melon.

"Why are you running so fast on such a hot day?" asked the girl.

"My yam talked to me!" exclaimed the farmer.

"My fish spoke, too!" said the fisherman.

The girl laughed so hard she almost dropped her melon. "I've never heard of anything so ridiculous!" she said.

"I agree," said the melon. "Everyone knows that yams can't talk."

The girl was so terrified that she actually *did* drop the melon. Then she ran away with the farmer and the fisherman as fast as her legs could carry her.

Up hill and down, they ran until they came to the King's hut.

The farmer stopped to catch his breath. "We must tell the King what is going on," he said.

"Yes," said the fisherman, puffing and panting. "The King is a wise man."

"He will know exactly what to do," said the girl.

The three rushed into the King's hut.

"My yam talked to me!" said the farmer.

The King gave the farmer a stern look. "Impossible," he said. "You have been working too long in the hot sun."

"My fish talked to me, too!" said the fisherman.

The King frowned. "Nonsense!" he exclaimed. "Your ears are playing tricks on you."

"And my melon talked to me!" the girl finally added.

The King became very angry. "Foolish tales like that could frighten the entire village," he roared. "Leave my hut immediately before I punish all of you severely!"

The farmer, the fisherman, and the girl wasted no time in leaving the king's hut. Foolish or not, they did not want to be punished.

The King sat back in his royal chair. He shook his head. "Thank goodness they are gone," he muttered to himself. "A talking yam indeed. I've never heard of anything so ridiculous."

"I agree," said his chair. "Everyone knows that yams can't talk!"

Name ______________________ Date ____________

Now answer Numbers 1 through 6. Base your answers on the story "The Talking Yam: An African Folktale."

1 Which word BEST describes the fisherman when the farmer tells him about the yam?

Ⓐ amused

Ⓑ happy

Ⓒ sad

Ⓓ scared

2 Read this sentence from the story.

Then he scrambled to his feet and ran on down the road, right on the farmer's heels.

What does the phrase *right on the farmer's heels* mean in the sentence above?

Ⓕ following the farmer very closely

Ⓖ moving past the farmer at a fast speed

Ⓗ attempting to trip the farmer, causing him to fall

Ⓘ keeping a great distance between himself and the farmer

3 What do the farmer, the fisherman, and the girl do about the talking objects?

Ⓐ They go to see the king.

Ⓑ They dive into the river.

Ⓒ They try to figure out why.

Ⓓ They decide that it is not true.

4 Read this sentence from the story.

The King gave the farmer a stern look.

What does the word *stern* mean in the sentence above?

Ⓕ beam

Ⓖ pleased

Ⓗ serious

Ⓘ stare

5 How are the farmer, the fisherman, and the girl all ALIKE?

Ⓐ They run when objects talk.

Ⓑ They are happy to see the king.

Ⓒ They do not believe that yams talk.

Ⓓ They think talking yams are funny.

6 What happens LAST in the story?

Ⓕ The girl drops her melon.

Ⓖ The king's chair talks to him.

Ⓗ The farmer runs down the road.

Ⓘ The fisherman throws the fish in the water.

Name ______________________ Date ____________

Read the article "The Truth About Bears" before answering Numbers 7 through 12.

The Truth About Bears

Three kinds of bears live in the United States. They are the black bear, the brown bear, and the polar bear.

Black Bears

Black bears are the most common of the three. They live in forests in many different parts of the country. Even though they are known as "black bears," they are not always black. Sometimes they are brown or tan, and a few are even white. Black bears are usually about five or six feet long. They are the smallest of the three kinds of bears.

Brown Bears

Brown bears are found in a few western states and in Alaska. They live in forests as well as in open areas called the tundra. Brown bears are usually light or dark brown and can grow to be very large. In fact, some are eight feet long!

Polar Bears

Polar bears can be found in Alaska, which is in a cold region near the North Pole called the Arctic, where there are no trees. Polar bears are white. They are the largest of the three kinds of bears. They are a little longer and usually heavier than the brown bear.

Other Interesting Things

Bears eat different things. Black and brown bears eat fish and other kinds of meat, roots, and berries. Polar bears eat fish, other meat, seaweed, and grass. All three types of bears eat as much food as they can find just before winter. Then during the cold months they sleep in caves or hollowed out trees called "dens," which keep them warm. Winter is when the female bears have their babies. All three types of bears have between one and four cubs. The cubs are born while the mother bear sleeps!

All people are afraid of bears. However, bears are actually shy. Most bears try to stay away from people, but still, bears can be dangerous at times. Mother bears do not want people to get too close to their babies, and bears do not want people to get close to their food!

Now answer Numbers 7 through 12. Base your answers on the article "The Truth About Bears."

7. What is the MAIN reason that the author wrote this article?

   Ⓐ to tell people not to feed bears

   Ⓑ to describe three kinds of bears

   Ⓒ to show how dangerous bears are

   Ⓓ to explain why bears sleep all winter

8. Where do polar bears live?

   Ⓕ near large forests

   Ⓖ near the North Pole

   Ⓗ in a few western states

   Ⓘ in many parts of the country

9. What do black bears, brown bears, and polar bears do BEFORE winter sets in?

   Ⓐ They sleep in dens.

   Ⓑ They feed their cubs.

   Ⓒ They eat as much food as they can.

   Ⓓ They move from forests into open areas.

Name ______________________ Date ______________

10 Read this sentence from the article.

Mother bears do not want people to get too close to their babies, and bears do not want people to get close to their food.

What does the word *close* mean in the sentence above?

Ⓕ block

Ⓖ end

Ⓗ near

Ⓘ shut

11 Which sentence from the article reveals the author's opinion, or point of view, about bears?

Ⓐ "Three kinds of bears live in the United States."

Ⓑ "Brown bears are found in a few western states and in Alaska."

Ⓒ "Bears eat different things."

Ⓓ "All people are afraid of bears."

12 Which section of the article tells the reader which kind of bear is most common?

Ⓕ Black Bears

Ⓖ Brown Bears

Ⓗ Polar Bears

Ⓘ Other Interesting Things

Name ________________________ Date ______________

Read the story "Strange Rain" before answering Numbers 13 through 18.

Strange Rain

Sedat sat on the edge of his bed looking out the window after the thunder had awakened him. He wasn't bothered much because he loved to watch storms. It was so dark and shadowy outside, though, that he could barely see out his window. As the storm continued, he heard an odd, thumping sound followed by what sounded like a bark. Then there was another thumping noise and what sounded like a meow. He decided to reach under his bed for his flashlight.

Sedat flipped the switch on the flashlight and pointed it toward the yard. All he could see was the glare from his window. He slipped out of his bed and opened the window and then heard more strange sounds. When he pointed his flashlight into the yard, he could not believe his eyes. It was raining cats and dogs!

Sedat rubbed his eyes and looked again. A cat landed softly on its feet and ran under a bush. A dog landed close by, and the cat jumped out. Then the two animals started to play.

Sedat saw his cat, Link, walking through the garden. Other cats and dogs rained down in the yard. Sedat worried that Link would disappear into the night with all of the other animals, so he put on his slippers and hurried down the stairs. He opened the back door and called out to Link and noticed that it was barely raining now. As he peered out at the darkness, he saw a cat moving toward him. He called Link's name again, and suddenly, Link ran inside and rubbed against Sedat's legs. Sedat dried Link gently with a towel, carried him upstairs, and fell asleep with his cat curled at the foot of the bed.

Sedat woke up early the next morning, and the sun was shining brightly. He dressed quickly and walked downstairs. His mother was opening the back door to go outside, and Sedat went out with her.

Name _______________ Date _______________

Sedat's mom looked at the garden. She propped up a flower pot that had been knocked over. Then she cut off a broken branch on another plant.

"Look how many plants were damaged during that powerful storm last night," she said. "It must have rained cats and dogs."

"Yes, it did," Sedat agreed. He smiled as Link rubbed against his legs and purred.

Name ____________________ Date ______________

Now answer Numbers 13 through 18. Base your answers on the story "Strange Rain."

13 Where does this story take place?

Ⓐ in a garden

Ⓑ in a basement

Ⓒ at Sedat's house

Ⓓ under Sedat's bed

14 Read this entry from a thesaurus.

> **bothered** *adj.* disturbed or troubled
> ***angry***
> ***embarrassed***
> ***hurt***
> ***upset***

Now read these sentences from the story.

> **Sedat sat on the edge of his bed looking out the window after the thunder had awakened him. He wasn't bothered much because he loved to watch storms.**

Which synonym is MOST LIKE the word *bothered* as it is used in the sentence above?

Ⓕ angered

Ⓖ embarrassed

Ⓗ hurt

Ⓘ upset

Name ______________________ Date ____________

15 What does Sedat do to show that he cares for Link?

Ⓐ He looks out the window.

Ⓑ He dries Link with a towel.

Ⓒ He watches Link in the yard.

Ⓓ He watches Link lick his paws.

16 Which word BEST describes Sedat?

Ⓕ curious

Ⓖ fearful

Ⓗ funny

Ⓘ grouchy

17 Read this sentence from the story.

"Look how many plants were damaged during that powerful storm last night," she said.

If *power* means "strong," what does the word *powerful* mean in the sentence above?

Ⓐ not strong

Ⓑ full of strength

Ⓒ in a strong way

Ⓓ without strength

18 Why does Sedat smile at the end of the story?

Ⓕ Link is safe inside the house.

Ⓖ His mother's garden is unharmed.

Ⓗ His mother goes outside with him.

Ⓘ It rained cats and dogs in his dream.

Read the article "Day and Night in the Desert" before answering Numbers 19 through 24.

Day and Night in the Desert

art by Paige Billin-Frye

In late spring, the desert is very hot and dry. But it is full of life. During the cool night, a beautiful saguaro cactus flower blossoms. In the morning, painted lady butterflies suck nectar from wildflowers growing in the sun.

Name ______________________ Date ______________

Nearby, a hungry lizard watches. It soon snaps up a butterfly and scurries away. Then it rests on a rock warmed by the sun. Lizards have to eat, too.

This western whiptail lizard has long claws to dig for food and catch insects.

A young snake slithers by, very quietly. It strikes quickly and gobbles up the lizard. The snake won't be hungry for the rest of the day.

Most desert animals stay hidden in the shade during the hot afternoon. But at sunset, the desert begins to cool. A roadrunner darts out from behind a barrel cactus. Roadrunners are very quick. The snake is a nice treat.

Roadrunners can't fly very well, so they run fast instead.

In the evening, a coyote waits in the darkness. It has begun its night of hunting to bring food to its family. It doesn't bother to chase the roadrunner. A roadrunner is very hard to catch. The coyote looks for a kangaroo rat instead.

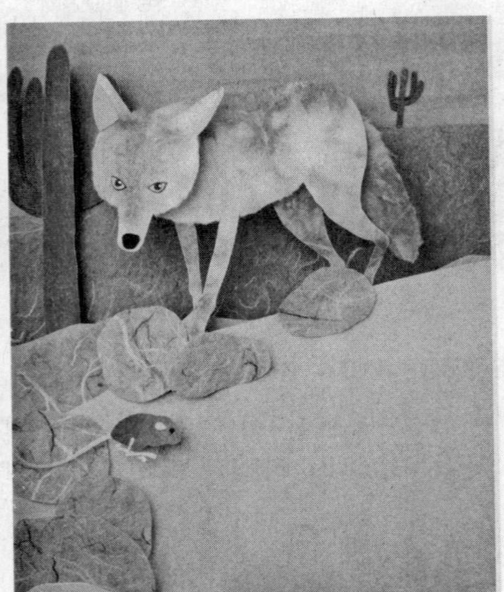

Under the desert moon, another saguaro flower blossoms. In the morning, a butterfly will sip nectar from wildflowers, and the search for food in the desert will begin again.

Name ______________________ Date ____________

Now answer Numbers 19 through 24. Base your answers on the article "Day and Night in the Desert."

19 What is the article MAINLY about?

Ⓐ what desert animals eat

Ⓑ how fast roadrunners can run

Ⓒ cactus flowers blooming at night

Ⓓ how plants and animals live in the desert

20 Read this sentence from the article.

In the morning, painted lady butterflies suck nectar from wildflowers growing in the sun.

What does the word *nectar* mean in the sentence above?

Ⓕ butterfly food

Ⓖ a type of fruit

Ⓗ a type of plant

Ⓘ butterfly shelter

21 Read these sentences from the article.

Nearby, a hungry lizard watches. It soon snaps up a butterfly and scurries away.

Why does the author use the phrase *snaps up* instead of *catches* in the sentence above?

Ⓐ to show how quickly the lizard grabs the butterfly

Ⓑ to show how the lizard uses its feet to catch the butterfly

Ⓒ to show how long it takes for the lizard to eat the butterfly

Ⓓ to show that the lizard is almost unable to catch the butterfly

Name ______________________ Date ______________

22 At what time of day is the desert the hottest?

Ⓕ at sunrise

Ⓖ early in the morning

Ⓗ in the afternoon

Ⓘ at sunset

23 Why do most desert animals stay hidden in the afternoon?

Ⓐ to sleep

Ⓑ to stay cool

Ⓒ to eat their prey

Ⓓ to hide from enemies

24 How does the author connect the ideas in the last paragraph to the ideas in the first paragraph?

Ⓕ The author describes how a cactus flower blossoms.

Ⓖ The author tells why it is difficult for animals to find food.

Ⓗ The author explains the nighttime activities of different desert animals.

Ⓘ The author tells what happens when night once again turns into morning in the desert.

Name _______________________ Date ___________

Read the articles "School News" and "We Were Here!" before answering Numbers 25 through 30.

School News

Science Section

Mrs. Torres's Science Class Finds Fossils

by: Amy Chang, Grade 3

Mrs. Torres is teaching about fossils, which are the remains of plants and animals that once lived. Mrs. Torres wanted to take her class to look for them. In December, the class went to Hogtown Creek, a nearby creek bed where Mrs. Torres knew many fossils had been found. The students started to explore the creek bed, spreading dirt and peering at rocks. They found many interesting things.

Jim Angelo was the first to find something. He showed his discovery to Mrs. Torres. She brought all of the students together to see what Jim found. It looked like part of a sand dollar embedded in a rock. Mrs. Torres said it had lived at the bottom of the sea hundreds, maybe thousands, of years ago. The stone may become Florida's state fossil. All of the students were excited about that.

Pilar Mendez was the next student to find a unique fossil. She found a stone with a line of tiny footprints fossilized across it. From the looks of the footprints, Mrs. Torres's class concluded that they were made by a very small bird. We all wondered where that little bird was going when it made those tracks so long ago.

Jessica Carlile found what appeared to be an odd-shaped stone. When she examined it more closely, though, she realized it was an actual shark's tooth—a very dirty one! Mrs. Torres washed it off. Jessica's brother Billy also found a shark's tooth. Mrs. Torres took the findings back to school.

It was a great day at Hogtown Creek. Students searched for fossils, which are very hard to find. It takes time to look for something so old and hidden. The fossils have all been cleaned. Now they all reside in Mrs. Torres's classroom. Her class welcomes everyone to come in and see them!

Name ______________________ Date __________

We Were Here!

A Guide to Fossils

Fossils are the remains of once-living animals and plants. Because of fossils, we know that dinosaurs and woolly mammoths once roamed the earth. Maybe they even wandered in your own backyard! Fossils of sea creatures on mountains tell us that oceans once covered these mountains. Fossils of tropical plants near the North and South Poles are evidence that these cold lands once had warmer climates. Studying fossils can tell us what life was like on earth long ago and how it has changed.

When most plants and animals die, they do not become fossils. Instead, they simply decay, or rot, and become part of the earth. Lucky for us, though, some turn into fossils. Others leave behind clues that say, "We were here!"

Fossils do not form overnight. It can take thousands of years for fossils to form. There are many ways that a plant or animal's remains can be preserved, or kept unchanged.

A common type of fossil is a stone fossil. A stone fossil forms when a plant or an animal's remains turn to stone over time. How does this happen? In wet places, after an organism dies, it is buried in mud. This often happens in a lake, river, or sea bed. Over thousands of years, layers of mud build up. The mud turns into rock. Water and minerals seep into the bones. Eventually, the bones are replaced with minerals and turn to stone. A stone fossil is formed!

When a tree or a piece of wood is replaced by minerals over time, it, too, can become a fossil. This type of fossil is called petrified wood.

Not all fossils turn into stone. Sometimes, feathers, animal tissue, and even plant seeds are preserved. In deserts and other dry places, bones, teeth, or claws may be preserved exactly as they are. Another way living things can become fossils is when they are trapped and preserved in frozen ground, tree sap, or even tar. Here are some fascinating examples:

- In 1901, the body of an ancient mammoth was discovered in Siberia. It was buried in the frozen ground. It had been there, unchanged, for ages!
- Sometimes leaves and insects can get stuck in tree sap. Over time, the sap hardens and turns into amber. Amber is fossilized tree sap. The amber preserves the organism inside.
- In some places around the world, the fossils of many large animals have been found in sticky tar pits. Once upon a time, these animals got stuck in the tar pits and died. The tar, or natural asphalt, preserved the animals' bones in a nearly perfect state.

Other fossils show us about animals' activities on earth. They show us how animals in the past lived and moved. These fossils include:

✓ *Tracks.* Tracks are animal footprints. Tracks can reveal much about the size and movements of animals.

✓ *Trails and burrows.* Trails are paths left by animals as they move across the earth. Burrows are holes or tunnels dug into the earth. Trails and burrows can tell us where animals lived and how they traveled.

✓ *Nests.* Some animals have left behind nests they built. The nests can contain clues about how the animals lived and cared for their young.

✓ *Tooth marks.* Animals can also leave behind tooth marks on objects they have chewed on. Tooth marks can tell us about an animal's eating habits.

Fossils are tiny slivers of a great puzzle. They help scientists piece together the earth's history. Next time you come across a fossil in a museum or in the woods, ask yourself some questions. What can it tell me about the organism it belonged to? What can it tell me about the earth's history?

Name ______________________ Date __________

Now answer Numbers 25 through 30. Base your answers on the articles "School News" and "We Were Here!"

25 According to the article "School News," who was the FIRST student to find a fossil?

Ⓐ Billy

Ⓑ Jessica

Ⓒ Jim

Ⓓ Pilar

26 Read this sentence from the article "School News."

The students started to explore the creek bed, spreading dirt and peering at rocks.

What does the word *peering* mean in the sentence above?

Ⓕ learning about

Ⓖ looking closely

Ⓗ throwing objects

Ⓘ trying to break apart

27 Read this sentence from the article "We Were Here!"

In wet places, after an organism dies, it is buried in mud.

What does the word *organism* mean in the sentence above?

Ⓐ a type of fossil

Ⓑ a plant or animal

Ⓒ a wet environment

Ⓓ a very large reptile

28 What is the author's MAIN purpose in writing the article "We Were Here!"?

Ⓕ to convince readers to look for and study fossils

Ⓖ to explain different types of fossils and how they form

Ⓗ to tell about where different fossils can be found on earth

Ⓘ to give interesting facts about dinosaur and mammoth fossils

29 What information is included in BOTH articles?

Ⓐ what a fossilized shark's tooth looks like

Ⓑ what happens after most plants and animals die

Ⓒ what tracks can show about the animal that made them

Ⓓ how an animal can be preserved inside an amber fossil

30 Which idea is included in the first paragraph of BOTH articles?

Ⓕ a definition of what fossils are

Ⓖ how a group went about searching for fossils

Ⓗ what scientists can learn from studying fossils

Ⓘ what interesting fossils might be found in a creek bed

Name ________________ Date ____________

Read the article "The Ferris Wheel" before answering Numbers 31 through 35.

The Ferris Wheel

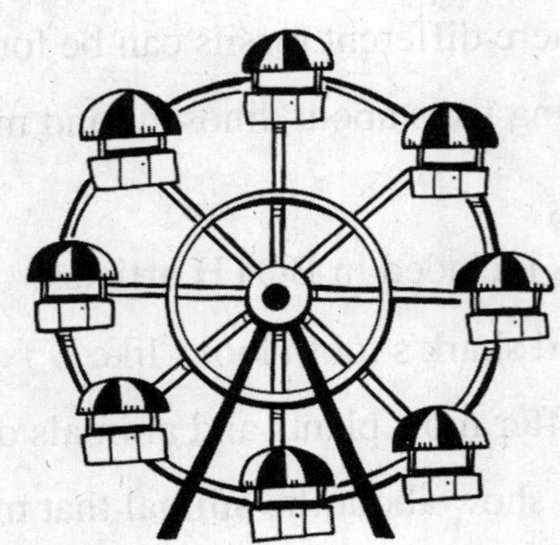

Have you ever gone on a Ferris wheel high above the city? Do you know who invented this giant wheel that goes round and round? It is an interesting story of a man with big ideas.

In 1892, George Ferris talked with the group of people who would run the World's Fair in Chicago. He showed them drawings of a giant wheel between two towers. The wheel looked like two bicycle wheels, but it was 26 stories high! That's as high as some tall city buildings.

Mr. Ferris told the group that the wheel would have thirty-six wooden cars on it, and each car would have forty chairs. People would sit in the chairs and ride while the wheel went around.

The members of the World's Fair group were uncertain about the wheel; it did not look safe for people, but Mr. Ferris assured them that he would not put people in danger. He was a bridge builder. He knew how to build safe bridges, and he knew how to make the wheel safe. The group consented to allow George Ferris to build his wheel for the fair.

Opening day of the Chicago World's Fair was in 1893. People who arrived were surprised to see the huge, tall wheel. The president of the fair introduced Mr. Ferris and his new ride, the Ferris wheel. Then Mr. Ferris, his wife, the mayor of Chicago, and many other people boarded the wheel.

They rode up above the city as the wheel turned. The view of the city was spectacular.

Everyone wanted to go on the new ride. It was a huge success. Mr. Ferris's big idea is still around. Ferris wheels today look very different from the first Ferris wheel, but the ride is still as much fun.

People from all over the world came to the Chicago World's Fair. Look at the chart to learn how long it would have taken visitors to get to Chicago.

Travel Times to Chicago in 1893

From	Estimated Travel Time
Berlin, Germany	11 days
Boston, Massachusetts	32 hours
Edinburgh, Scotland	10 days
London, England	9-1/2 days
Mexico City, Mexico	5 days
Montreal, Quebec, Canada	29 hours
New Orleans, Louisiana	36 hours
New York, New York	26 hours
San Francisco, California	3-1/2 days
St. Petersburg, Russia	16 days
Vienna, Austria	11 days

Name ______________________ Date ____________

Now answer Numbers 31 through 35. Base your answers on the article "The Ferris Wheel."

31 Read this sentence from the article.

Then Mr. Ferris, his wife, the mayor of Chicago, and many other people boarded the wheel.

What does the word *boarded* mean in the sentence above?

Ⓐ to get on

Ⓑ to sit down

Ⓒ to stand up

Ⓓ to walk away

32 Which of the following BEST tells how the author feels about Ferris wheels?

Ⓕ They are fun.

Ⓖ They are unsafe.

Ⓗ They are boring.

Ⓘ They are curious.

33 Why were people at the fair surprised to see the big wheel?

Ⓐ It was so enormous.

Ⓑ It looked too dangerous.

Ⓒ It was in the middle of the fair.

Ⓓ It was not supposed to be built.

Name ________________________ Date ____________

34 According to the chart, from which place did it take the longest to get to Chicago?

Ⓕ Vienna, Austria

Ⓖ Berlin, Germany

Ⓗ Edinburgh, Scotland

Ⓘ St. Petersburg, Russia

35 According to the chart, from which two places did it take the same amount of time to get to Chicago?

Ⓐ Berlin, Germany and Vienna, Austria

Ⓑ London, England and San Francisco, California

Ⓒ New Orleans, Louisiana and New York, New York

Ⓓ Boston, Massachusetts and Montreal, Quebec, Canada

STOP

Name ______________________ Date ____________

Revising and Editing

Read the introduction and the story "Juan Becomes a Cook" before answering Numbers 1 through 5.

Juan wrote this story about a meal he made for his friends. Read his story and think about the changes he should make.

Juan Becomes a Cook

(1) I had been telling my friends about how much I like to cook. (2) The truth is, I've never really cooked anything. (3) I only knows how to make sandwiches.

(4) Last Saturday, my friends, Hector and Sammy, were at my house playing basketball. (5) Suddenly everyone was hungry. (6) Sammy said, "Hey, Juan, you like to cook. (7) Will you make us some lunch?"

(8) How could I say no? (9) I hurryed into the kitchen. (10) I looked in the pantry and the refrigerator. (11) Then I stopped to think for a minute. (12) Suddenly something occurred to me. (13) First, I grabbed some leftover cooked beans, apple slices, shredded cheese, lettuce, and dry cereal. (14) Then I threw in some spices that looked interesting. (15) I crushed the cereal with a rolling pin and mixed it into the beans, along with the apple slices and spices. (16) I put the mixture inside each lettuce leaf. (17) Finally, I topped it with shredded cheese and rolled up the lettuce.

Name ______________________ Date ____________

(18) "What are these?" asked Hector when I served lunch.

(19) "The'yre good," said Sammy.

(20) Hector nodded. (21) "I guess you really do like to cook!" he said.

(22) What I am is a lucky cook! (23) I think I will stop stretching the truth.

Now answer Numbers 1 through 5. Base your answers on the changes Juan should make.

1. Which sentence could BEST be added at the beginning of this story?
   - Ⓐ My friends and I like to play basketball.
   - Ⓑ I like to make sandwiches for my friends.
   - Ⓒ My friends asked me to cook a meal for them.
   - Ⓓ Sometimes you get into trouble by stretching the truth.

2. What change should be made in sentence 3?
   - Ⓕ change ***knows*** to **know**
   - Ⓖ change ***make*** to **made**
   - Ⓗ change ***sandwiches*** to **sandwichs**
   - Ⓘ change the period to a question mark

3. What change should be made in sentence 9?
   - Ⓐ change ***I*** to **I'd**
   - Ⓑ change ***hurryed*** to **hurried**
   - Ⓒ change ***kitchen*** to **Kitchen**
   - Ⓓ change the period to a question mark

Name ______________________ Date ____________

4 What time-order word could BEST be added to the beginning of sentence 16?

Ⓕ First,

Ⓖ Finally,

Ⓗ Later,

Ⓘ Next,

5 What change should be made in sentence 19?

Ⓐ change ***The'yre*** to **They're**

Ⓑ change the comma to a question mark

Ⓒ change ***said*** to **say**

Ⓓ change ***Sammy*** to **sammy**

Name _______________________ Date ___________

Read the introduction and the article "What Is Wind?" before answering Numbers 6 through 10.

Jenna wrote this article about wind. Read her article and think about the changes she should make.

What Is Wind?

(1) What is wind? (2) What causes it? (3) When the sun shines on land and water, they warms them as well as the air above them. (4) The warm air becomes lighter. (5) As a result, it rises. (6) Then, cooler air rushes in to replace the rising warm air. (7) This movement creates wind.

(8) Earth's surface does not heat evenly. (9) As a result, wind blows constantly. (10) Land heats and cools more quickly than water, so air is always moving between land and water. (11) Places on earth also heat up and cool down at different

Name ______________________ Date ______________

rates, causing air to move between the hot and cold places.

(12) Over time, wind can shape rocks and landscapes. (13) It blows away tiny pieces of rock. (14) As a result, wind can reshape mountains. (15) The small, loose pieces of rock often form into sand dunes.

(16) People have learned to use the power of wind. (17) For example, they uses it to sail ships, dry clothes, and fly kites. (18) Many citys use wind power to generate electricity.

(19) We can't see wind, but we can feel it, see it's effects, and put it to good use. (20) Day after day, wind was changing our world.

Now answer Numbers 6 through 10. Base your answers on the changes Jenna should make.

6. What change should be made in sentence 3?
   - Ⓕ change ***shines*** to **shine**
   - Ⓖ remove the comma after ***water***
   - Ⓗ change ***they*** to **it**
   - Ⓘ change ***air*** to **are**

Name ______________________ Date ____________

7 What change should be made in sentence 17?

Ⓐ change ***uses*** to **use**

Ⓑ change ***sail*** to **sale**

Ⓒ remove the comma after ***clothes***

Ⓓ change ***kites*** to **kite**

8 What change should be made in sentence 18?

Ⓕ change ***citys*** to **cities**

Ⓖ change ***use*** to **uses**

Ⓗ add a comma after ***wind***

Ⓘ change ***electricity*** to **Electricity**

9 What change should be made in sentence 19?

Ⓐ change ***can't*** to **ca'nt**

Ⓑ remove the comma after ***effects***

Ⓒ change ***put*** to **puts**

Ⓓ change ***it's*** to **its**

10 What change should be made in sentence 20?

Ⓕ remove the comma after ***wind***

Ⓖ change ***was*** to **is**

Ⓗ change ***our*** to **are**

Ⓘ change the period to a question mark

STOP

Name ________________________ Date ______________

Writing to Inform

Read the prompt and plan your response.

> **Most people have a person in their life who they admire, or look up to.**
>
> **Think about someone in your life who you admire.**
>
> **Now write to explain why you admire, or look up to, this person.**

Planning Page

Use this space to make your notes before you begin writing. The writing on this page will NOT be scored.

Name ______________________ Date ____________

Begin writing your response here. The writing on this page and the next page WILL be scored.

Name ______________________ Date __________

Writing to Inform

Name ______________________ Date __________

Reading Complex Text

Read the article "Dialing into the Future." As you read, stop and answer each question. Use evidence from the article to support your answers.

Dialing into the Future

Let's say a visitor from the past drops in on you today. She arrives straight from the year 1984. She lands on a busy street in the town where you live. It is a Saturday, and people are out enjoying their weekend. She strolls down the street, amazed. There are so many strange and unfamiliar things!

Here is something this time traveler has never seen before. Many people are holding little rectangles up to their ears. Even stranger, they're talking into them.

"What on earth are they doing?" she asks. "Who or what are they talking to?"

You happen to be walking by so you try to explain. First, you tell her that they are not talking into little rectangles. They are talking on their cell phones, a kind of telephone.

1. Why does the author use the word *you* in the article?

____

____

____

Now, a telephone is a device this time traveler knows well. In 1984 telephones had been around for 108 years. They were invented in 1876 by Alexander Graham Bell. Back then, they hardly looked the way they do now.

Much larger and heavier than the cell phones of today, telephones would either sit on a flat surface or attach to the wall. To make a call, you picked up the receiver, which was usually attached to a base by a stretchy, coiled cord. Phone numbers were dialed by putting your finger in the hole of a wheel and spinning it. Later, numbered buttons, like those on a cell phone, replaced the wheel.

Talking to people is only one of the things that you can do on a cell phone. On some cell phones, you can send and receive written messages, listen to music, and watch movies. You can also read books, play games, and use maps. The list gets longer every day.

As you explain all that you know, the time traveler's eyes seem about to pop. She is so surprised that you can't help but continue.

You tell her that the cell phone combines different kinds of technology that she already knows about. Much of it existed in 1984. Some of it comes from a hundred years before.

One of these technologies is the radio. A cell phone is really a kind of radio. Nikolai Tesla invented the radio in the 1880s, not long after the invention of the telephone.

2. Based on the article, how are telephones DIFFERENT from cell phones?

____

____

____

Radios work by sending invisible waves through the air. These waves travel 186,000 miles every second, the same speed as light. They can carry sounds, images, and other information from one cell phone to another.

Radio waves are used in many devices that we use often. They are used in radios and televisions. They are also used in microwave ovens, garage-door openers, and walkie-talkies.

In order to make a call to someone else in the world, your cell phone needs to send a message to the nearest cell phone tower. This message is sent to the tower using radio waves. Then the tower, or another tower like it, sends the message to the other person's phone. This last step is also done with radio waves.

Cell phone towers are spread out around the country. They pick up the waves that are closest to them. The area in which each tower operates is called a cell.

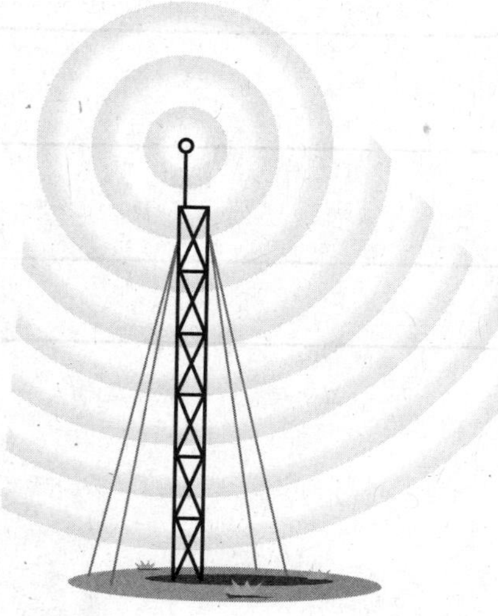

Name _______________ Date _______________

3 Explain how radio waves allow cell phones to make calls.

Cell phones are a lot more complicated than radios, you begin telling your time-traveling friend. The tiny computers inside cell phones, for example, once took up a whole room. But you decide that for now, this is enough for the time traveler to know.

That's when you realize that you have a question for her! How did she get to the future anyway? After all, even now there's still no such thing as time travel, except in books and movies!

4 Why does the narrator compare new technology to old technology? Provide an example that supports your answer.

Name ______________________ Date ______________

Reading and Analyzing Text

Read the story "Cody and Friends Make a Difference" before answering Numbers 1 through 18.

Cody and Friends Make a Difference

"Mom! Please don't throw away that bottle!" Cody called to his mother. He was seated at the kitchen table, writing on sheets of paper.

"What should I do with it, then?" Mom asked Cody.

"You should recycle it," said Cody. "That way it can be used again. If you throw it away, it'll become more trash."

"How did you become so wise about these things?" Cody's mom asked, taking a seat beside him at the table.

"We're learning about recycling at school," he answered. "The less we throw away, the less trash ends up in landfills or in the environment. Trash and pollution are global problems, and solving these problems begins with each one of us."

Cody continued, "We can reuse a lot of what we throw away. Used plastics can be made into all sorts of things such as rope and toys. Glass bottles and jars can be cleaned and used again, or they can be crushed and used in other products. Old newspapers can be made into cartons and bags."

"You're right," said Mom. "All of that is true."

"Then why were you going to throw away the bottle?" Cody asked.

"Our town doesn't have a recycling program," said Mom. "The city council doesn't think enough people would take advantage of it."

"I'll bet that a *lot* of people would recycle if we had a program. Someone ought to convince the city council to start one," said Cody. "I can't do it, though, because I'm just a kid," he said with a note of disappointment in his voice. He returned to his writing.

"What are you working on?" asked Mom.

"I'm writing a book report on *Charlotte's Web*," said Cody.

Cody's mother smiled. "Charlotte the spider saves Wilbur the pig," she said. "That is a great book whose story shows that even a small creature can make a huge difference."

Cody looked up from his writing. "Wait! Who says I can't make a difference just because I'm a kid? If a spider can save a pig's life, maybe anything's possible. There might be a way for me to start a recycling program after all. I could get my friends to help with the project."

"That's a great idea, Cody!" said Mom. "The next town meeting is in three weeks. You and your friends could make a presentation there. You could have your friends meet at our house this Saturday to make a plan."

On Saturday, twelve of Cody's friends met at his house. They discussed ways to make a presentation. There would be a lot of work, so they divided it into groups. Cody and some friends would write a letter asking the council to start a recycling program. Then, they would ask the town's residents to sign the letter. Others would prepare pictures, charts, and graphs to use during the presentation. Another group would gather things made from recycled materials to show what recycling could do. Finally, everyone would try to get neighbors and family members to come to the meeting.

When the night of the town meeting arrived, the friends were a little nervous. "Now we will hear a presentation from some of the town's younger residents," announced the mayor. Cody presented the letter he and his friends had written along with several pages of signatures. The other children explained their pictures, charts, and graphs and showed examples of objects made from recycled materials.

A month later, there was another town meeting. After the meeting, the mayor announced that the council had voted to start a recycling program. No one was more excited than Cody. The children's parents had a pizza party to celebrate. Cody gave a speech in which he thanked his friends for their help. At the end of his speech, he said,

Name ______________________ Date ____________

"Now I know that even a kid can make a difference, and twelve kids can make a *big* difference!"

Now answer Numbers 1 through 18. Base your answers on the story "Cody and Friends Make a Difference."

1. How is Cody's mom throwing away a bottle important to the story's plot?

   Ⓐ It shows that Cody's mom doesn't know what it means to recycle.

   Ⓑ It starts a conversation between Cody and his mom about recycling.

   Ⓒ It leads to an argument between Cody and his mom about recycling.

   Ⓓ It shows how much trash winds up in landfills and the environment.

2. How does Cody FIRST learn that the town doesn't have a recycling program?

   Ⓕ from the mayor, while at a town council meeting

   Ⓖ from his teacher, while learning about recycling at school

   Ⓗ from his friends, who have started recycling programs in other towns

   Ⓘ from his mom, who explains why she was going to throw the bottle away

Name ______________________ Date __________

3 Read this sentence from the story.

"Trash and pollution are global problems, and solving these problems begins with each one of us."

What does the word *pollution* mean in the sentence above?

Ⓐ new ways to use trash

Ⓑ trash that was put in landfills

Ⓒ people who work to make a better world

Ⓓ waste that makes air, land, or water dirty

4 Read this sentence from the story.

"Trash and pollution are global problems, and solving these problems begins with each one of us."

What does the word *global* mean in the sentence above?

Ⓕ difficult

Ⓖ modern

Ⓗ serious

Ⓘ worldwide

5 Read this sentence from the story.

"We can reuse a lot of what we throw away."

What does the word *reuse* mean in the sentence above?

Ⓐ use up

Ⓑ use again

Ⓒ use before

Ⓓ use one time

Name ______________________ Date __________

6 Read this sentence from the story.

Old n<u>ew</u>spapers can be made into cartons and bags.

Which word has the same sound as the underlined part of the word *newspapers*?

Ⓕ blueberry

Ⓖ daughter

Ⓗ powerful

Ⓘ unlawful

7 Read this sentence from the story.

"The city coun<u>c</u>il doesn't think enough people would take advantage of it."

Which word has the same sound as the underlined part of the word *council*?

Ⓐ bucket

Ⓑ candle

Ⓒ chicken

Ⓓ simple

8 How does Cody and his mom's conversation about *Charlotte's Web* help develop the story's plot?

Ⓕ It helps Cody realize that he should reach out to his friends for help.

Ⓖ It gives background on Cody and his mother's shared love of reading.

Ⓗ It helps Cody realize that he can try to start a recycling program in his town.

Ⓘ It gives Cody's mom the idea that they should start a recycling program.

Name ______________________ Date ____________

9 Read this sentence from the story.

"I could get my friends to help with the project."

What does the word *project* mean in the sentence above?

Ⓐ party to celebrate

Ⓑ contest on recycling

Ⓒ report on what happens

Ⓓ plan for work to be done

10 What lesson does Cody take away from *Charlotte's Web* and apply to his own life?

Ⓕ that he should try to save the lives of animals

Ⓖ that friends should always help each other out

Ⓗ that even small creatures can have an important impact

Ⓘ that spiders are living creatures and should be protected

11 What is the FIRST thing that Cody and his friends do before they start work on their presentation?

Ⓐ They divide the work into groups.

Ⓑ They write a letter to the town council.

Ⓒ They prepare pictures, charts, and graphs.

Ⓓ They gather things made from recycled materials.

Name ____________________ Date __________

12 Read this sentence from the story.

Others would prepare pictures, charts, and graphs to use during the presentation.

Which word has the same sound as the underlined part of the word *prepare*?

Ⓕ card

Ⓖ fair

Ⓗ hear

Ⓘ part

13 Read this sentence from the story.

Finally, everyone would try to get neighbors and family members to come to the meeting.

What does the word *finally* mean in the sentence above?

Ⓐ in the middle

Ⓑ as a last thing

Ⓒ without change

Ⓓ lasting a long time

14 Read this sentence from the story.

"Now we will hear a presentation from some of the town's younger residents," announced the mayor.

If the word *reside* means "live in a particular place," what does the word *residents* mean as used in the sentence above?

Ⓕ people who live in a particular place

Ⓖ people who live in several different places

Ⓗ people who do not wish to live in a particular place

Ⓘ people who live in a particular place for a short time

Name _______________________ Date _______________

15 Read this sentence from the story.

The other children explained their pictures, charts, and graphs, and showed examples of objects made from recycled materials.

Which of these shows the correct way to divide the word *children* into syllables?

Ⓐ chi • ldren

Ⓑ ch • ildren

Ⓒ chil • dren

Ⓓ childr • en

16 Read these sentences from the story.

After the meeting, the mayor announced that the council had voted to start a recycling program. No one was more excited than Cody. The children's parents had a pizza party to celebrate.

Which words from these sentences help the reader know what the word *celebrate* means?

Ⓕ had voted

Ⓖ was excited

Ⓗ the children's parents

Ⓘ had a pizza party

17 How is the MAIN problem in the story solved?

Ⓐ The town council votes to start a recycling program.

Ⓑ Cody and his friends give a presentation to the town council.

Ⓒ Cody reaches out to his friends to help him with a presentation.

Ⓓ Cody decides what to write for his book report on *Charlotte's Web*.

18 Which line from story BEST conveys the story's central theme, or message?

Ⓕ "Finally, everyone would try to get neighbors and family members to come to the meeting."

Ⓖ "Cody presented the letter he and his friends had written along with several pages of signatures."

Ⓗ "Cody gave a speech in which he thanked his friends for their help."

Ⓘ "'Now I know that even a kid can make a difference, and twelve kids can make a *big* difference!'"

Name ______________________ Date ______________

Read the journal entries in "My Week as a Fossil Hunter" before answering Numbers 19 through 35.

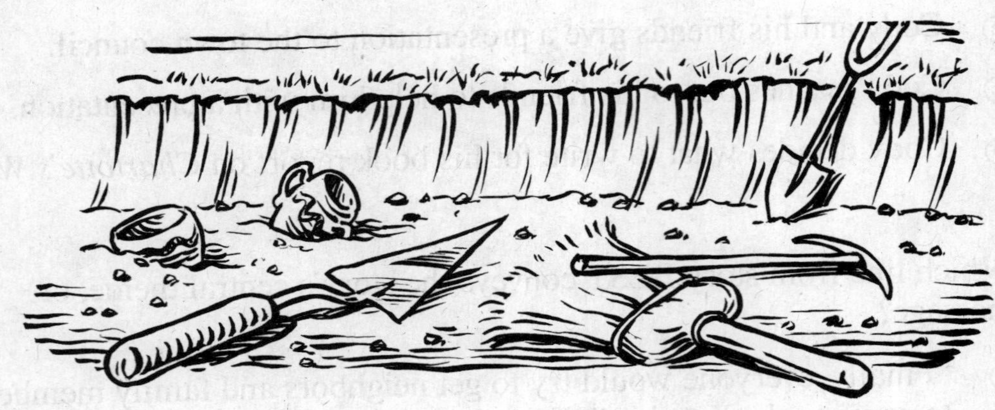

My Week as a Fossil Hunter

Sunday, June 5

A dream has come true for me. Ever since I was five years old, I've been interested in dinosaurs. Now I have the chance to look for dinosaur bones. Tomorrow morning, I'll be helping a team of students dig for fossils—and not just dinosaurs.

We're at a ranch in northern New Mexico. The climate is dry, the days are warm, and the nights are cool. There are cliffs, hills, and mountains. It is a beautiful part of the country. The dig site where I'll be working is called Hayden Quarry.

In the past few years, scientists and other researchers have found remains of dinosaurs and fish and traces of other animals at the quarry. Thousands of animal bones are buried under the rock here. These bones and other objects tell us much about life long ago.

I hope I'm able to sleep tonight. I'm excited for tomorrow to be here. Who knows what we may dig up?

Name ____________________ Date __________

Monday, June 6

The first thing we have to do in our area is remove the rock that covers the fossils. This rock is called the overburden. It comes from ancient rivers that flowed through the area.

We worked all day using shovels to remove the rock. Halfway through our work, the sounds of a distant thunderstorm rumbled from far away. Our leader moved us to safety for a few hours. When the thunder stopped, we got back to work.

I asked our group leader how people knew to dig for fossils in this location. He told me that a hiker walking through here in 2002 discovered some fossils. After that, people who collect and study fossils began to come here to look for bones, teeth, and other prehistoric remains.

I must remember to take some pictures. The sunlight on the cliffs is so pretty!

Tuesday, June 7

Now that the rock layer is out of the way, we're using small picks and brushes to remove rock and dirt around the bones we find. We have to be very careful not to damage the bones as we uncover them. Some of the tools we use aren't much bigger than a toothpick!

I'm too tired to write any more tonight, but I loved every minute of today. The hard work and hot sun wore me out. It did help that I wore my hat and plenty of sunscreen. I wish I could stay for a whole month instead of just one week.

Wednesday, June 8

Today, one of the students found the upper leg bone of a dinosaur. Everyone was pretty excited about that discovery. I got to touch the bone with my hands! How many people get to do that?

The fossils we've been finding are very different in size. The fossils can be as tiny as a grain of sand or longer than one foot. To find the smaller fossils, we have to scoop up clumps of dirt and put them in bags that have very tiny holes. Next we put the bags in a nearby stream, under big rocks to hold them in place. The water washes the

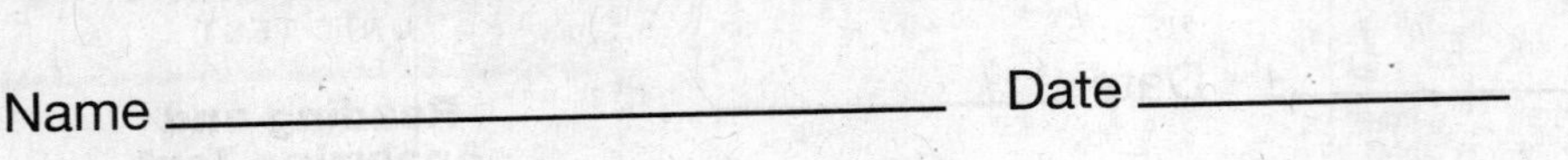

Name ______________________ Date ______________

mud away. Then we dry what's left on a sheet in the sun. This makes it easier to find the smaller fossils.

I'm learning so much and having fun doing it. Maybe I'll do this for a living someday.

Thursday, June 9

So far our team has found six bones! I am on top of the world about this! It really is amazing that we have found so many. Usually it takes months to find that many bones at one site.

All of the fossils will be sent to a lab. People at the lab will carefully study the fossils for clues. These clues tell them what animal the fossils belonged to, what it looked like, how it moved, and what it ate.

The bad news is that I am going home in two days. The good news is, when I get back home, I'll have lots of great stories and pictures to share with my family and friends.

Now answer Numbers 19 through 35. Base your answers on the journal entries in "My Week as a Fossil Hunter."

19. What does the title of the journal help the reader to know?

  Ⓐ that the writer is a girl
  Ⓑ that the writer is in New Mexico
  Ⓒ that these are notes about looking for fossils
  Ⓓ that these are notes about camping out in June

20 Read this sentence from the journal.

The dig site where I'll be working is called Hayden Quarry.

What does the word *site* mean in the sentence above?

Ⓕ an area or place

Ⓖ an enclosed room

Ⓗ a dry environment

Ⓘ a wooden platform

21 Read these words from the journal.

In the past few years, scientists and other researchers have found remains of dinosaurs and fish and traces of other animals at the quarry.

Which word from the sentence above helps the reader understand the meaning of *researchers*?

Ⓐ scientists

Ⓑ remains

Ⓒ dinosaurs

Ⓓ animals

Name ______________________ Date ______________

22 Read the dictionary entry below.

traces \trās'ĕz\ *noun* **1.** lines. **2.** signs. **3.** straps. **4.** trails.

Read this sentence from the journal.

In the past few years, scientists and other researchers have found remains of dinosaurs and fish and traces of other animals at the quarry.

Which meaning BEST fits the way the word *traces* is used in the sentence above?

Ⓕ meaning 1

Ⓖ meaning 2

Ⓗ meaning 3

Ⓘ meaning 4

23 Read this sentence from the journal.

Thousands of animal bones are buried under the ro<u>ck</u> here.

Which word has the same sound as the underlined part of the word *rock*?

Ⓐ camp

Ⓑ chin

Ⓒ knife

Ⓓ voice

24. Why are the people at Hayden Quarry digging for fossils?

Ⓕ so they can enjoy time outdoors

Ⓖ so they can compare sizes of fossils

Ⓗ so they can learn about life long ago

Ⓘ so they can sell the fossils to make money

25. Read this sentence from the journal.

I asked our group leader how people knew to dig for fossils in this location.

What does the word *location* mean as used in the sentence above?

Ⓐ ground

Ⓑ place

Ⓒ town

Ⓓ way

26. How has the author organized the information in this journal?

Ⓕ by types of fossils

Ⓖ by days of the week

Ⓗ in order of importance

Ⓘ from last to first event

Name ______________________ Date ____________

27 Read this sentence from the journal.

After that, people who collect and study fossils began to come here to look for bones, teeth, and other prehistoric remains.

What does the word *prehistoric* mean in the sentence above?

Ⓐ related to history

Ⓑ after written history

Ⓒ before written history

Ⓓ the early part of history

28 Read this sentence from the journal.

Now that the rock layer is out of the way, we're using small picks and brushes to rem<u>o</u>ve rock and dirt around the bones we find.

Which word has the same sound as the underlined part of the word *remove*?

Ⓕ good

Ⓖ spoon

Ⓗ took

Ⓘ wool

29 Read this sentence from the journal.

Some of the tools we use aren't much bigger than a toothpick!

Which of the following tells the correct way to divide the word *toothpick* into syllables?

Ⓐ too • thpick

Ⓑ too • th • pick

Ⓒ tooth • pick

Ⓓ tooth • pi • ck

Name ______________________ Date ____________

30 Read this sentence from the journal.

To find the smaller fossils, we have to scoop up clumps of dirt and put them in bags that have very tiny holes.

What does the word *clumps* mean in the sentence above?

Ⓕ bags and tubs

Ⓖ signs and fossils

Ⓗ rocks and stones

Ⓘ lumps and clusters

31 Read these sentences from the journal.

So far our team has found six bones! I am on top of the world about this!

Why does the author use the phrase *on top of the world* in the sentence above?

Ⓐ to show that she feels happy about her team's finds

Ⓑ to show that her team found the bones high in the mountains

Ⓒ to show that she believes her team members are the best diggers

Ⓓ to show how hard she and her team members have been working

32 Read this sentence from the journal.

People at the lab will carefully study the fossils for clues.

If *careful* means "thorough," what does the word *carefully* mean in the sentence above?

Ⓕ not thorough

Ⓖ mostly thorough

Ⓗ in a thorough way

Ⓘ able to be thorough

Name ____________________ Date ______________

33 Read this sentence from the journal.

People at the lab will carefully study the fossils for clues.

What does the word *clues* mean in the sentence above?

Ⓐ bones

Ⓑ hints

Ⓒ marks

Ⓓ pictures

34 Which sentence from the journal tells the reader that the dig at Hayden Quarry has been uncommon for scientists?

Ⓕ "A dream has come true for me."

Ⓖ "All of the fossils will be sent to a lab."

Ⓗ "The fossils we've been finding are very different in size."

Ⓘ "Usually it takes months to find that many bones at one site."

35 How does the author's experience at Hayden Quarry affect her point of view about dinosaurs and fossils?

Ⓐ She wasn't interested in dinosaurs and fossils until she went to Hayden Quarry.

Ⓑ She wants to study dinosaurs and fossils, but now she wants to do it from inside a lab.

Ⓒ She always liked dinosaurs and fossils, and now she is considering studying them for a living.

Ⓓ She learns a lot about dinosaurs and fossils, but now she wants to study something different.

Name ______________________ Date ____________

Revising and Editing

Read the introduction and the story "Rolling on the River" before answering Numbers 1 through 5.

Kevin wrote this story in which he describes an experience. Read his story and think about the changes he should make.

Rolling on the River

(1) Have you ever weared a boat? (2) When my family and I was planning a trip to a kayak camp last summer, I learned about kayaks. (3) I found out that you actually wear them!

(4) A kayak is a type of boat, usually for one person. (5) Kayaks for the sea are long and thin, and kayaks for rivers are short and wide. (6) Our kayaks were river kayaks.

(7) Before you get into a kayak, you put on clothes that help to keep you warm and dry. (8) One piece of clothing is a skirt. (9) The skirt is rubbery. (10) The skirt fastens to a lip on the kayak to help keep water out of the boat. (11) After putting on the skirt, you squeeze into the kayak and attach it. (12) This makes you feel like you're wearing the kayak. (13) For safety reasons, you also need to wear a helmet.

Name ______________________ Date ____________

(14) For the first two days of camp, we learned what to do in case we tip. (15) We did rolls under water, using our paddle to roll back on top of the water. (16) We practiced these rolls in a swimming pool. (17) On the third day, we paddled in our kayaks on the calm part of the river.

(18) Onse I got the hang of paddling, it was fun. (19) Each day, we learned more about kayaking and paddled our boats on more fast water. (20) I liked the thrill of being on a fast-moving river. (21) I tipped over into the river twice, but both times I rolled right back up!

Now answer Numbers 1 through 5. Base your answers on the changes Kevin should make.

1. What change should be made in sentence 1?
   - Ⓐ change ***Have*** to **Has**
   - Ⓑ change ***you*** to **you've**
   - Ⓒ change ***weared*** to **worn**
   - Ⓓ change the question mark to a period

2. What change should be made in sentence 2?
   - Ⓕ change ***and*** to **or**
   - Ⓖ change ***was*** to **were**
   - Ⓗ change ***learned*** to **learn**
   - Ⓘ change ***kayaks*** to **kayak**

Name ______________________ Date __________

3 What is the BEST way to combine sentences 8 and 9?

Ⓐ One piece of clothing is a rubbery skirt.
Ⓑ One piece of clothing is a skirt rubbery.
Ⓒ One piece of clothing is a skirt, a rubbery skirt.
Ⓓ One piece of clothing is a skirt, the skirt is rubbery.

4 What change should be made in sentence 18?

Ⓕ change ***Onse*** to **Once**
Ⓖ change ***I*** to **me**
Ⓗ add a comma after ***hang***
Ⓘ change ***was*** to **is**

5 What change should be made in sentence 19?

Ⓐ change ***we*** to **they**
Ⓑ change ***more*** to **most**
Ⓒ change ***paddled*** to **paddle**
Ⓓ change ***more fast*** to **faster**

Name ____________________ Date __________

Read the introduction and the story "A Favorite Day at School" before answering Numbers 6 through 10.

Jennifer wrote this story about a favorite experience at school. Read her story and think about the changes she should make.

A Favorite Day at School

(1) We're learning about Italy in class. (2) Since food is an important part of life in Italy, our teacher invited a chef from an Italian restaurant to come to class. (3) The chef showed us how to make fresh pasta.

(4) The chef began by mixing together flour, salt, and eggs to make pasta dough. (5) She kneaded the dough by folding and pressing firmly it down. (6) She covered the dough in plastic wrap and let it rest for a while. (7) Next, she divided the dough into eight pieces and gave one piece to each pair of students.
(8) Each pair had a metal pasta roller with a hand crank.
(9) We put a piece of dough in one end and cranked it through.
(10) What came out was a strip of dough. (11) It was flat. (12) We could change the roller setting to make the dough thinner and thinner. (13) When the strip were just right, the chef cut it into smaller strips, like ribbons. (14) Then she boiled the ribbons.
(15) I used to think all pasta came from a box. (16) I couldn't have been more wrong. (17) Welcome to homemade spaghetti!

Name ______________________ Date ____________

Now answer Numbers 6 through 10. Base your answers on the changes Jennifer should make.

6 What is the BEST way to revise sentence 5?

Ⓕ She kneaded the dough by folding and pressing it down firmly.

Ⓖ She kneaded firmly the dough by folding and pressing it down.

Ⓗ She kneaded the dough by firmly folding it and firmly pressing it down.

Ⓘ She kneaded the dough by, firmly folding it, and then pressing it down, firmly.

7 Which transition word could BEST be added to the beginning of sentence 6?

Ⓐ After,

Ⓑ Although,

Ⓒ Then,

Ⓓ Sometimes,

8 What is the BEST way to combine sentences 10 and 11?

Ⓕ What came out was a flat strip of dough.

Ⓖ What came out was a strip of dough, flat.

Ⓗ What came out was a strip of dough, it was flat.

Ⓘ What came out was a strip of dough and a flat dough.

9 What change should be made in sentence 13?

Ⓐ change ***were*** to **was**

Ⓑ remove the comma after ***right***

Ⓒ change ***smaller*** to **smallest**

Ⓓ change ***ribbons*** to **ribons**

Name ______________________ Date ____________

10 Where is the BEST place in the story to begin a new paragraph?

Ⓕ sentence 3

Ⓖ sentence 7

Ⓗ sentence 14

Ⓘ sentence 15

Name ______________________ Date ______________

Writing Opinions

Read the prompt and plan your response.

> **Exercise is an important part of a healthy life.**
>
> **Think about some reasons why it is important to get some exercise each day.**
>
> **Now write to persuade other third graders that it is important to get some exercise each day.**

Planning Page

Use this space to make your notes before you begin writing. The writing on this page will NOT be scored.

Name ______________________ Date ____________

Begin writing your response here. The writing on this page and the next page WILL be scored.

Name ______________________ Date ____________

Name ______________________ Date ______________

Reading Complex Text

Read the article "Adventures of an Aquanaut." As you read, stop and answer each question. Use evidence from the article to support your answers.

Adventures of an Aquanaut

If you wanted to become an explorer today, where could you go? European explorers of the past sailed off in search of new continents. They discovered Asia, Africa, and North and South America. Later explorers discovered the North and South Poles. They navigated icy waters and frozen land to reach those remote places. For the modern explorer, it might feel like everywhere on earth has already been discovered.

You might think you have to travel to space to discover new places. However, there is somewhere much closer to home, and it covers most of the earth. It's the ocean. The ocean is deeper than anyone has ever been able to go. In some places the ocean is seven miles deep, which leaves most of it unexplored.

Just ask Sylvia Earle, underwater explorer or "aquanaut." Diving down deep below the ocean's surface, Earle has seen spectacular seascapes. She has visited underwater mountain ranges, plains, and caverns. She has explored places no sunlight reaches.

1. What does the word *explorer* mean as used in the section above?

____

____

____

Diving into the ocean, says Sylvia Earle, is "like falling into a galaxy of little stars or the Fourth of July fireworks." Brilliantly colored fish and plants light up this world like fireflies. You can come face to face with whales as big as school buses. You can see giant 1800-pound tunas and beautiful seahorses and dolphins.

Name _______________________ Date ___________

Earle has discovered plants and animals no one ever knew existed. She has dived deeper than almost anyone else.

Her adventures, however, have shown her that the ocean is in trouble. People once thought the ocean was so large it would never get too polluted or run out of fish. But people are eating or destroying more fish than the ocean can replace. They are putting too many chemicals into the ocean and taking out too many fish. Many of these fish are gone forever. Others are very close to being gone.

2 Why are many fish gone or close to being gone forever?

____

____

____

The ocean makes life on earth possible for all living things, in the sea and on land. Much of the air we breathe is made by tiny plants in the ocean. The ocean also shapes the earth's climate and weather.

When fish disappear, this affects the whole ocean. It eventually affects us, too. Take sharks as just one example. So many sharks have been fished out of the ocean that in some places they are gone forever. This means that some of what the sharks eat have gotten too numerous. Since sharks eat jellyfish, for example, parts of the ocean now have too many jellyfish. This causes problems for many smaller fish. Jellyfish eat a large amount of organisms called plankton. Smaller fish also eat plankton. Because there are more and more jellyfish, now many smaller fish cannot get enough plankton to survive. This affects the humans who rely on the smaller fish as a food source.

3 What problem does overfishing of sharks cause for smaller fish?

____

____

____

This chain reaction goes on and on. It moves from humans, to sharks, to jellyfish, to smaller fish and plankton, and back to us. What we do affects the ocean. And if the ocean is in trouble, so are we.

4 What is the main idea of this article? What details does the author provide to support the main idea?

____

____

____

____

____

Name ______________________ Date ____________

Reading and Analyzing Text

Read the story "Anna's Adventure" before answering Numbers 1 through 6.

Anna's Adventure

Anna dressed in her new pants, tucked in her shirt, and brushed her hair. After she looked in the mirror and decided she was ready, she ran into the room where her parents were sitting.

"You look so lovely," her mother complimented her, smiling.

"Thank you," Anna said. "Can we leave now? I don't want to be late."

"Are you excited about seeing your favorite writer?" her father asked.

Anna grinned and nodded. Everyone knew how long she had been waiting for this day. She had read all the books written by Ms. Black and had even read some of them twice.

Ms. Black was a well-known writer who wrote mostly mysteries. Although the books were like written puzzles, Anna could usually untangle the mystery before the main character in the book did.

Anna and her parents drove to the bookstore, and fortunately, there was little traffic. Anna was surprised but pleased that they had arrived early because they found seats close to the front. All the chairs were taken soon after they got there. The crowd was composed mostly of young boys and girls, and everyone was discussing Ms. Black and their favorite books.

The crowd became still when the owner of the bookstore walked out. He welcomed everyone warmly and then mentioned there was a small problem. Anna wondered what the hold-up might be.

"It seems Ms. Black is not here," he told the crowd.

Everyone seemed disappointed. Anna was perplexed at first, but then she remembered the plot of one of Ms. Black's books. In the book, the main character was a writer, and the writer disappeared. Anna tried to remember what had happened in the book and began glancing around the

Name ______________________ Date ____________

room. A few other children seemed to understand that Ms. Black might not really be missing after all.

Anna stood up and announced, “We have a mystery. Ms. Black is missing, so let’s figure out where she is.”

The bookstore owner smiled, and the younger children in the crowd calmed down. Anna and the older children formed a group and began talking about where Ms. Black could be.

“What happened in Ms. Black’s book about the disappearing writer?” Anna asked.

One of the children replied, “The writer got lost in the library.”

“Should we try to find her at the library?” another child asked.

“I think maybe she’s here at the bookstore. Maybe she’s lost among the books here,” Anna suggested. “Let’s go look in the section where the mysteries are.”

The children walked through the bookstore. Sure enough, sitting comfortably among the mysteries was Ms. Black, and she was reading a book. The children gathered around her in excitement. She told them what a good job they had done, and then she followed them into the room where everyone else was waiting. The crowd clapped when they saw her, and Ms. Black smiled proudly.

“Thank you all for being here. I’m sorry I was late, but I suppose I got a little lost. Perhaps you could clap again for the children who solved tonight’s first mystery,” Ms. Black said.

The crowd applauded again and then settled in to listen to Ms. Black read from her latest book.

Name ____________________ Date __________

Now answer Numbers 1 through 6. Base your answers on the story "Anna's Adventure."

1. Where does this story MOSTLY take place?

   Ⓐ a library

   Ⓑ a bookstore

   Ⓒ Anna's house

   Ⓓ a writer's house

2. Read this sentence from the story.

   The crowd was composed mostly of young boys and girls, and everyone was discussing Ms. Black and their favorite books.

   What does the word *composed* mean in the sentence above?

   Ⓕ sat in order

   Ⓖ waited quietly

   Ⓗ made up of

   Ⓘ listened carefully

3. What happens RIGHT AFTER the bookstore owner says that Ms. Black is missing?

   Ⓐ Anna decides she is ready.

   Ⓑ The crowd seems let down.

   Ⓒ Anna and her parents leave.

   Ⓓ The bookstore owner smiles.

Name ______________________ Date ______________

4 How does Anna help solve the mystery?

Ⓕ Anna calls out Ms. Black's name.

Ⓖ Anna helps to calm down the younger children.

Ⓗ Anna tells the crowd to look for Ms. Black in the library.

Ⓘ Anna remembers Ms. Black's book about a missing writer.

5 Why does Ms. Black tell the children that they did a good job?

Ⓐ They are able to find her.

Ⓑ They come to listen to her speak.

Ⓒ They read all of Ms. Black's books.

Ⓓ They help calm down the young kids.

6 Read this sentence from the story.

The crowd applauded again and then settled in to listen to Ms. Black read from her latest book.

What does the word *latest* mean in the sentence above?

Ⓕ oldest

Ⓖ longest

Ⓗ most recent

Ⓘ most famous

Read the article "The Running Farmers" before answering Numbers 7 through 12.

The Running Farmers

Copper Canyon is located in Mexico. It is a large group of canyons, or deep valleys, that got its name from the copper-colored plants that grow on its walls. Copper Canyon is bigger and deeper than the Grand Canyon.

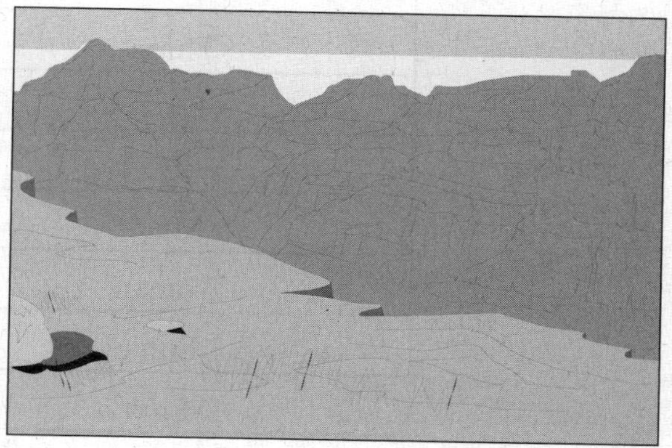

A group of Indians called the Raramuri live there today. Hundreds of years ago, different people moved into the area near Copper Canyon. The Raramuri wanted to be alone, so they moved to more hidden places. They moved deep into the canyons where many of them still live. Some live there part of the year and move to the top of the canyon for the rest of the year. They go back and forth to farm certain crops. Near the top of the canyon, they grow apples and peaches. In the canyons, they grow oranges and corn, which are their main foods.

It is hard to grow crops in Copper Canyon because the soil is not very good. For this reason, farms are far apart. The Indians have to find land where crops will grow. Homes are also far apart, so the Indians must travel a long way to work and to visit.

Raramuri means "foot runners." They seem to run nonstop! They run between their farms and their homes, and they run when they are herding their goats. They run when they are hunting, and they run when they carry supplies. They also play a game where teams kick a ball as they run. These races can last for days.

Some of the Raramuri Indians have entered running races in other parts of the world. All of the other runners wear professional running shoes. Sometimes the Raramuri wear running shoes, but other times they wear simple sandals. The bottoms of those sandals are made out of old tires, and still, the Raramuri can win the race!

Name ______________________ Date __________

Tarahumara, also known as Raramuri, is a language of Mexico. There are more than 60,000 Tarahumara speakers in Mexico. Look at the chart to learn some Tarahumara words.

English Word	Tarahumara Word
One	Biré
Two	'Osá
Three	Bikiyá
Four	Nawó
Five	Marí
Man	Rihóy
Woman	'Upí
Sun	Rayénari
Moon	Micá

Now answer Numbers 7 through 12. Base your answers on the article "The Running Farmers."

7. Why did the Raramuri move deeper into Copper Canyon?

   Ⓐ They did not know where else to live.

   Ⓑ They did not want other people around.

   Ⓒ They saw how beautiful the canyon was.

   Ⓓ They knew it would be easy to grow crops there.

8. Why is it difficult for the Raramuri to grow crops?

   Ⓕ The soil is quite poor.

   Ⓖ The canyon is so deep.

   Ⓗ The Raramuri move often.

   Ⓘ The Raramuri live far apart.

9 Read this sentence from the article.

They seem to run nonstop!

What does the word *nonstop* mean in the sentence above?

Ⓐ stop again

Ⓑ unable to stop

Ⓒ before stopping

Ⓓ without stopping

10 What is the MAIN reason the author wrote this article?

Ⓕ to give information about the Raramuri Indians

Ⓖ to tell a story about a Raramuri Indian who won a race

Ⓗ to describe the difficulty of farming near Copper Canyon

Ⓘ to show that Copper Canyon is bigger than the Grand Canyon

11 According to the chart, what is the Tarahumara word for *moon*?

Ⓐ Bikiyá

Ⓑ Marí

Ⓒ Micá

Ⓓ Rayénari

12 According to the chart, what does the Tarahumara word *'Upí* mean?

Ⓕ five

Ⓖ four

Ⓗ man

Ⓘ woman

Name ______________________ Date ____________

Read the stories "Come On, Raj!" and "That Time Again" before answering Numbers 13 through 18.

Come On, Raj!

"Come on, Raj!" Neela called. Her head bobbed up and down, up and down, as she tread water. Raj stood at the end of the dock, looking longingly at his best friend. He wagged his tail and whined, pacing back and forth. How refreshing the lake looked, he thought. The August sun shined down on Raj's brown-and-white, spotted fur, making him pant. But no matter how many times Raj approached the edge of the dock and got into leaping position, his paws refused to budge. No sir, his paws said. We are staying on firm ground!

For the past half an hour, Neela had been swimming in the lake with her friends. She was splashing around and having a grand time. She called out encouraging words to her dog, tempting him with a tennis ball, his favorite toy! Still, Raj couldn't summon the courage to leave the end of the dock and jump in the lake.

The sweeter Neela spoke to him, the more he felt like he was letting her down. He was afraid she was going to give up on him and turn her attention to her friends. It was August after all, which meant *that time* again. School would start in just a few weeks. One morning, Neela would wake up and, instead of heading outside together, she would pat Raj on the head and wave goodbye. Then, she would board that big yellow monster to join her other friends. The bus, as it was called, would roar away down the street. Neela would be gone—well, gone until late afternoon, anyway.

Raj couldn't bear the thought of losing any more fun time with Neela. No matter how hard his paws tried to hold him back, he *had* to jump in the water. Raj sat back on his haunches to try and collect himself. He let out his deepest, heartiest "WOOF!" Then he stood up on all fours. He walked backward a few steps. Then he walked forward a few steps. Finally, he sprung off the dock into the air.

Squeezing his eyes shut, Raj braced himself for the landing. Splash! His head ducked under the warm water just for a moment before

surfacing. "Way to go, Raj!" Neela cheered. "You did it!" If dogs could smile, Raj would have just then. He paddled toward his best friend. He had done it! And the water was just as refreshing as he imagined it would be. When Raj reached Neela, he swam circles around her in celebration. She laughed. She told him, "I'm so proud of you, Raj! I knew you could find the courage to jump in. We're going to have such a fun afternoon swimming together in the lake." And they did just that.

Name ______________________ Date ____________

That Time Again

A week later, Raj wandered into Neela's bedroom one evening. He hoped to find his best friend sprawled on her bed, reading a mystery or drawing. Raj had just eaten. He was ready to curl up next to Neela and fall asleep. From time to time, Neela would even reach over and scratch behind his ears.

Instead of finding Neela on her bed, however, Raj found her scurrying around her room. He stood in the doorway and watched her. She pulled her favorite dress out of her closet and held it up in front of her. Then, Neela turned to her desk. She grabbed a brand-new notebook and set of pencils and stuffed them into her bright green backpack. Backpack . . . Backpack . . . Raj tried to recall when he had last seen that backpack. Suddenly, he remembered. It was several months ago. Neela took that backpack back and forth from school. Oh, no! School!

Raj's brown ears drooped. He pulled his tail between his legs. The last few weeks, Raj and Neela had spent every waking hour together. They played fetch in the park, snoozed in the backyard, and swam at the lake. But now that dreaded time had come again. It was September. School was beginning again. Neela turned and spotted Raj. He let out a gloomy *Woof*!

"Oh, Raj, I know how you hate this time of year. I promise it won't be so bad. Just think about the nice long nap you can have after I leave in the morning. When I get home in the afternoon, you'll be ready to play!" Neela patted Raj's head, but Raj didn't feel any better. When Neela began chattering about all of the changes third grade would bring, Raj felt even worse. Surely, Neela would make all sorts of new friends and forget all about him!

The next morning, Raj dragged himself downstairs with Neela. He sat next to her as she ate her cereal. He watched her sadly as she rifled through her backpack to make sure she had all of her supplies. Then, Neela kissed her mother's cheek and headed for the front door. She called, "Bye, Mom! I don't want to miss the bus on the first day!" Raj's worst fear had come true. In her rush to get to school, Neela had already forgotten him. Raj hung his head. He had never felt more lonesome in his whole life.

Raj retreated to a patch of sunshine under the living room window. He shrunk down in the warm spot, but even the sunshine couldn't cheer him up. Suddenly, the front door burst open. Neela bounded into the house. "Raj, I forgot to say goodbye to you! I'm so sorry. Can you forgive me?" Neela asked. She knelt down next to him and rubbed his head. "I'll be home before you know it," Neela told him. Raj licked Neela's hand. His tail thumped happily against the floor, telling her she was already forgiven! Neela gave him one last scratch behind the ear before darting out the front door once again.

Raj stretched out and closed his eyes, feeling the warm sun on his back. Maybe this school thing won't be so bad after all, he thought as he yawned. After playing all summer long, taking a nap sounded good to Raj. So he did just that.

Now answer Numbers 13 through 18. Base your answers on the stories "Come On, Raj!" and "That Time Again."

13. Which of the following MOST motivates Raj to jump into the water in "Come On, Raj!"?

   (A) the hot sun and the prospect of cooling off in the water

   (B) Raj's favorite toy – a tennis ball – that Neela is waving at him

   (C) Neela calling to Raj to join her

   (D) the idea of not being able to have fun with Neela when summer ends

14. How does the illustration in "Come On, Raj!" help you understand Raj's character?

   (F) It shows why he is nervous about jumping in the water.

   (G) It shows how much he does not want to disappoint Neela.

   (H) It shows how happy he is when finally jumps into the lake.

   (I) It shows how much Raj doesn't want Neela to go back to school.

Name ______________________ Date ____________

15 Read this sentence from the story "That Time Again."

Instead of finding Neela on her bed, however, Raj found her scurrying around her room.

Why does the author use the word *scurrying* instead of *moving*?

Ⓐ to show how busy Neela is

Ⓑ to show that Neela is ready to relax

Ⓒ to show where Neela is in her bedroom

Ⓓ to show that Neela has been waiting for Raj

16 What happens right after Neela leaves the house for the FIRST time in "That Time Again"?

Ⓕ Raj goes downstairs.

Ⓖ Neela's mom pats Raj.

Ⓗ Raj feels sad and lonesome.

Ⓘ Raj yawns and goes to sleep.

17 Who is telling the story in "Come On, Raj!" and "That Time Again"?

Ⓐ Raj

Ⓑ Neela

Ⓒ a narrator who can show Raj's thoughts

Ⓓ a narrator who can show Neela's thoughts

Name ______________________ Date ____________

18 How do the settings of "Come On, Raj!" and "That Time Again" DIFFER?

Ⓕ "Come On, Raj!" takes place at a lake. "That Time Again" takes place at Neela's house.

Ⓖ "Come On, Raj!" takes place in a park. "That Time Again" takes place at Neela's school.

Ⓗ "Come On, Raj!" takes place at a pool. "That Time Again" takes place in Neela's backyard.

Ⓘ "Come On, Raj!" takes place in Neela's bedroom. "That Time Again" takes place in Neela's kitchen.

Name ______________________ Date ____________

Read the article "Wonderful Bones" before answering Numbers 19 through 24.

Wonderful Bones

Do you know how many bones are located in your body? When you were a baby, you had about 330 bones. Now you have just over 200 bones. The number decreases because some bones join together as you grow. Your wonderful bones work together to protect you and support your body.

Many Uses

Many bones protect your body. For example, the bone that makes up your head is called the skull. The skull surrounds your brain and protects it from harm. The ribs that cover your chest protect your heart and lungs.

Other bones are used to support the body. The many bones in your feet allow you to walk and stand on your tiptoes. Finger bones move together so that you can throw a ball or tie a bow. Your hands and feet have more than half of the bones in your body! When you think of all that you do with your hands and feet, it's a good thing they have so many bones.

Biggest Bone

The longest and strongest bone in your body is in your leg. It is called the femur. It goes from your hip to your knee. It is a very important bone because it carries all of your weight and helps you move from place to place.

Smallest Bone

Would you believe the smallest bone in your body is in your ear? It is about the size of a grain of rice and is called the stirrup. It is called that because it is shaped like a tiny loop and looks like a stirrup on a saddle. When sound waves come into your ear, the stirrup shakes back and forth, allowing the sound waves to reach your brain. When the waves reach your brain, you hear the sound.

"Funny" Bone

Hah! The funny bone isn't really a bone at all. It is actually a nerve. When you hit the nerve that is near your elbow, it really hurts or tingles. What's so funny about that? The funny bone probably got its name from the bone that is above your elbow. That bone is called the humerus, which sounds like the word *humorous,* meaning "funny."

The bones that make up our bodies are big, small, and in-between sized. They help us grow, protect us, and allow us to move. When you think about it, our bones really are wonderful.

Now answer Numbers 19 through 24. Base your answers on the article "Wonderful Bones."

19. What is the article MAINLY about?

   Ⓐ how the funny bone got its name

   Ⓑ why we have fewer bones as adults

   Ⓒ how different bones help our bodies

   Ⓓ why the longest bone helps us move

20. Which section explains how the bones in your feet help you?

   Ⓕ Many Uses

   Ⓖ Biggest Bone

   Ⓗ Smallest Bone

   Ⓘ Funny Bone

21. In what way are the skull and ribs ALIKE?

   Ⓐ They both support the body.

   Ⓑ They are both found in the chest.

   Ⓒ They both allow the body to move.

   Ⓓ They both protect other body parts.

Name ______________________ Date ______________

22 Read this sentence from the article.

They help us grow, protect us, and allow us to move.

What does the word *protect* mean in the sentence above?

- Ⓕ allow
- Ⓖ guard
- Ⓗ stand up for
- Ⓘ watch over

23 Which sentence from the article reveals the author's OPINION, or point of view, about bones?

- Ⓐ "Finger bones move together so that you can throw a ball or tie a bow."
- Ⓑ "The longest and strongest bone in your body is in your leg."
- Ⓒ "Would you believe the smallest bone in your body is in your ear?"
- Ⓓ "When you think about it, our bones really are wonderful."

24 According to the author, why are bones so wonderful?

- Ⓕ Some make us laugh.
- Ⓖ They send sound waves.
- Ⓗ Some look like other things.
- Ⓘ They protect and support us.

Name ______________________ Date ____________

Read the story "Rainbow Trout's Colors" before answering Numbers 25 through 30.

Rainbow Trout's Colors

by Robert James Challenger
illustrated by Susan Kwas

Grandfather and his grandson were working outside, bringing in the winter firewood. The day was dull and rainy, and as they worked the cold water ran down their necks.

The grandson said, "I wish it would never rain. I like the clear sky and the warm sun better."

Grandfather looked at him and said, "Let's take a rest and I'll tell you a story about the rain."

They found a dry spot under Cedar Tree to sit, and Grandfather began.

Down in the lake, Trout once felt the same way you do. He liked summer's sun because food became more plentiful. This is when the water in the lake gets warm and the insects hatch.

One rainy day, Trout saw Eagle flying overhead and called out to him, "Eagle, can you fly up into the sky and drag the rain clouds away to the other side of the mountain?"

Eagle asked, "So you think it would be good for the rain to go away so you could have sun all the time?"

"Oh, yes," said Trout. "It would be warm and bright and there would be lots of food for me."

Eagle thought, "It looks like I need to teach Trout a lesson."

Eagle flew up into the sky and dragged the grey rain clouds to the next valley, letting the bright sun shine down on Trout's lake.

Trout was very happy. Every day was bright, warm, and cheerful, and there was lots to eat. But after a while things started to change. Trout noticed that the water in the lake was not as deep as it used to be. The lake was getting smaller, leaving nothing but dry mud in its place. Trout also noticed that the insects, who needed the water to feed and hatch their eggs, had left. As the water got lower there was less to eat and Trout was finally trapped in a little pond with no food and barely enough room to turn around.

Trout looked up and saw Eagle watching him from a treetop. Trout called out, "Eagle, I was wrong. There can be too much sunshine. Now I know that rain is an important part of our world. Without it, the lake and everything I need to live will go away."

Eagle flew over the mountain and dragged the clouds back. Just before they covered over the sun, a bright rainbow came down from the rain clouds and shone on Trout. The colors splashed onto his scales and changed him into Rainbow Trout.

Grandfather looked up into the sky and said to his grandson, "I accept the cloudy weather, just like Rainbow Trout now does, because I know that without rain there would never be rainbows. Remember, everything has a purpose, even though we may not always understand what it is."

Now answer Numbers 25 through 30. Base your answers on the story "Rainbow Trout's Colors."

25 Where does Grandfather tell his story?

Ⓐ in a boat

Ⓑ near a lake

Ⓒ under a tree

Ⓓ on a mountain

26 Read this sentence from the story.

Remember, everything has a purpose, even though we may not always understand what it is.

What does the word *purpose* mean in the sentence above?

Ⓕ idea

Ⓖ matter

Ⓗ object

Ⓘ reason

27 How are Trout and Eagle DIFFERENT?

Ⓐ Trout noticed all the things around him, but Eagle did not.

Ⓑ Eagle did not have the power to stop the rain, but Trout did.

Ⓒ Trout did not at first understand what is good about the rain, but Eagle did.

Ⓓ Eagle was not bothered whether it rained or not, but Trout knew he needed rain.

Name ______________________ Date ______________

28 What happens to Trout when there is no more rain?

Ⓕ Trout's lake becomes dry, and there is no food.

Ⓖ Trout enjoys the sunny days and never complains.

Ⓗ Trout's life gets easier because there is so much food.

Ⓘ Trout decides to thank Eagle for taking the clouds away.

29 Which word BEST describes Grandfather?

Ⓐ careful

Ⓑ hard-working

Ⓒ joyful

Ⓓ wise

30 What lesson does Eagle teach Trout?

Ⓕ The clouds can be taken to another place.

Ⓖ The sunshine brings food and warm water.

Ⓗ Both sunshine and rain are necessary to live.

Ⓘ It is best when everything is warm and bright.

Read the poem "My Grandma Said" before answering Numbers 31 through 35.

My Grandma Said

My Grandma is wise
With sparkly brown eyes,
And she told me this,
"Hurt no living thing,
My dear little miss."

Let the beautiful butterfly fly.
Let the wild cat cry.
Let the baby chick cheep.
Let the stinky bug creep.
Hurt no living thing.

Pick no pretty wildflower;
Let it grow and tower
Over other tiny plants.
Cut no vine or rose,
For each one grows
In its dark, warm home of dirt.

Each animal and plant that is green
Should be left to be seen
By others who will delight
In their animal ways,
In their green plant sways,
In all of their beauty so bright.

They are beautiful, like us.
And so we must
Never hurt any living thing.

Name ______________________ Date ____________

Now answer Numbers 31 through 35. Base your answers on the poem "My Grandma Said."

31 According to the poem, why should wildflowers NOT be picked?

- (A) so people can enjoy looking at them
- (B) so they will not spread
- (C) so their green plants can sway
- (D) so they can be food for animals

32 Who is the narrator in this poem?

- (F) a plant
- (G) Grandma
- (H) a butterfly
- (I) a granddaughter

33 Read this line from the poem.

Let the wild cat cry.

Now complete the analogy below. Base your answer on what the word *cheep* means.

Wild cat* is to *cry* as ________ is to *cheep.

Which word BEST completes the analogy?

- (A) butterfly
- (B) baby chick
- (C) stinky bug
- (D) pretty wildflower

Name ______________________ Date __________

34 Read these lines from the poem.

Each animal and plant that is green
Should be left to be seen
By others who will delight
In their animal ways,

What does the word *delight* mean in the line above?

Ⓕ enjoy

Ⓖ forget

Ⓗ live

Ⓘ need

35 Which BEST describes the author's purpose in writing this poem?

Ⓐ to express an idea about how to treat living things

Ⓑ to entertain the reader with a funny story about nature

Ⓒ to convince the reader to get outdoors and enjoy nature

Ⓓ to inform the reader about how plants and animals grow

STOP

Name ______________________ Date ____________

Revising and Editing

Read the introduction and the story "The Word Game" before answering Numbers 1 through 5.

Felicia wrote this story about playing a word game with her friends. Read her story and think about the changes she should make.

The Word Game

(1) Last week, Allie, Jan, Meena, and I played a word game. (2) We used small letter tiles to make words in crossword patterns. (3) For each word, we added up the points for each letter to figure out the word's score. (4) Once we had used up all of our letters, the game was over.

(5) I played with Jan on one team against Allie and Meena on another. (6) After a few rounds, the two teams was tied. (7) Then, on Meena's turn, she spelled the word *triplop*.

(8) "If *triplop* is really a word, what does it mean?" I asked.

(9) "It means to gallop and trip at the same time," Meena answered weak.

(10) "You can't gallop *and* trip!" I said, giggling.

(11) Jan searched the dictionary for the word and finally announced, "*Triplop* is not in the dictionary!" (12) We all laughed, including Meena. (13) Near the end of the game, Meena tryed to use the word *qwerty* to win the game.

(14) "That's the sillier made-up word you've ever played!" Jan said. (15) Meena just smiled and handed Jan the dictionary. (16) When Jan found the word, everyone except Meena was surprised. (17) With the points from *qwerty,* Allie and Meena won the game.

Now answer Numbers 1 through 5. Base your answers on the changes Felicia should make.

1. Which sentence could BEST follow and support sentence 4?
   - Ⓐ Jan lives down the street from Meena.
   - Ⓑ The letters have points that go with them.
   - Ⓒ My friends and I like to ride bicycles together.
   - Ⓓ The team with the highest score would win the game.

2. What change should be made in sentence 6?
   - Ⓕ change ***rounds*** to **rownds**
   - Ⓖ change ***teams*** to **team**
   - Ⓗ change ***was*** to **were**
   - Ⓘ change ***tied*** to **tyed**

3. What change should be made in sentence 9?
   - Ⓐ change ***It*** to **she**
   - Ⓑ change ***and*** to a comma
   - Ⓒ change ***answered*** to **answer**
   - Ⓓ change ***weak*** to **weakly**

Name ______________________ Date ____________

4 What change should be made in sentence 13?

Ⓕ change ***Near*** to **Neer**

Ⓖ change ***of*** to **on**

Ⓗ change ***tryed*** to **tried**

Ⓘ change the period to a question mark

5 What change should be made in sentence 14?

Ⓐ change ***That's*** to **Thats'**

Ⓑ change ***sillier*** to **silliest**

Ⓒ change ***you've*** to **youve**

Ⓓ remove the quotation mark after ***played***

Read the introduction and the story "Plan B" before answering Numbers 6 through 10.

Marcus wrote this story about his visit to a science museum. Read his story and think about the changes he should make.

Plan B

(1) Plan A, our picnic at the park, was cancelled because of rain. (2) Mom said, "Let's try Plan B." (3) Our family always has a backup plan in case the first plan doesn't work out.

(4) Plan B was a visit to the Barger Science Museum. (5) The museum is one of my favorite places. (6) You can see dinosaur bones, experience what it's like to be an astronaut, and take a make-believe journey through the solar system. (7) There are many other things to do at the museum, too.

(8) Dad and I visited an exhibit and the exhibit made us feel like we were in a fierce windstorm. (9) Later, my sister, Kayla, and I created music that was so good, other museum visitors applauded when they heard it!

(10) Kayla and Mom walked through the museums butterfly garden. (11) Dad and I watched bees in their glassed-in hive. (12) We also watched a short film about how bees use danceing to communicate.

Name ______________________ Date ______________

(13) "I could spend a whole week at the science museum" Kayla said on the way home. (14) "I think it should be our Plan A *and* Plan B all the time!" (15) "That was the better rainy day ever!" I said.

Now answer Numbers 6 through 10. Base your answers on the changes Marcus should make.

6. What is the BEST way to rewrite sentence 8?
   - Ⓕ Dad and I visited an exhibit, made us feel like we were in a fierce windstorm.
   - Ⓖ Dad and I visited an exhibit that made us feel like we were in a fierce windstorm.
   - Ⓗ Dad and I visited an exhibit and it make us feel like we were in a fierce windstorm.
   - Ⓘ Dad and me visited an exhibit and the exhibit made us feel like we were in a fierce windstorm.

7. What change should be made in sentence 10?
   - Ⓐ change ***Mom*** to **mom**
   - Ⓑ change ***walked*** to **walk**
   - Ⓒ change ***through*** to **during**
   - Ⓓ change ***museums*** to **museum's**

8. What change should be made in sentence 12?
   - Ⓕ change ***watched*** to **wached**
   - Ⓖ change ***bees*** to **bee's**
   - Ⓗ change ***danceing*** to **dancing**
   - Ⓘ change the period to a question mark

9. What change should be made in sentence 13?
   - Ⓐ change ***spend*** to **spended**
   - Ⓑ change ***whole*** to **hole**
   - Ⓒ add a comma after ***museum***
   - Ⓓ remove the quotation mark after ***museum***

10. What change should be made in sentence 15?
    - Ⓕ change ***was*** to **were**
    - Ⓖ change ***better*** to **best**
    - Ⓗ change the exclamation mark to a period
    - Ⓘ add a quotation mark after ***said***

Name ______________________ Date ____________

Read the introduction and the article "Roots & Shoots" before answering Numbers 11 through 15.

Tamara wrote this article about a program to protect earth. Read her article and think about the changes she should make.

Roots & Shoots

(1) Have you ever watched a plant grow? (2) If so, you know that a network of roots holds a plant in the soil, and a tiny, green shoot is the first sign of a new plant's life. (3) With out roots and shoots, plants could not grow.

(4) That's what Jane Goodall imagineed when she began the Roots & Shoots program in 1991. (5) Goodall believes that even the most young citizens can help change the world. (6) Through Roots & Shoots, kids learn to spot problems in their communities and think of ways to solve them. (7) Kids, teens, parents, and teachers can all work on service projects together. (8) Special events teach people how to care for earth.

Name ____________________ Date __________

(9) Young people all around the world are joining Roots & Shoots programs. (10) In some cities, kids are planting trees. (11) In others, they're volunteering at local zoos and animal shelters. (12) One kids are helping to design earth-friendly shopping bags. (13) "No matter how many problemes we face," says a teen volunteer, "there is still hope as long as kids like us continue to care."

Now answer Numbers 11 through 15. Base your answers on the changes Tamara should make.

11 What change should be made in sentence 3?

Ⓐ change ***With out*** to **Without**

Ⓑ add a comma after ***roots***

Ⓒ change the comma to a period

Ⓓ change ***plants*** to **Plants**

12 What change should be made in sentence 4?

Ⓕ change ***That's*** to **Thats**

Ⓖ change ***Jane*** to **jane**

Ⓗ change ***imagineed*** to **imagined**

Ⓘ change ***in*** to **below**

Name ______________________ Date ______________

13 What change should be made in sentence 5?

Ⓐ change ***believes*** to **believe**

Ⓑ change ***most young*** to **youngest**

Ⓒ change ***help*** to **helping**

Ⓓ change the period to a question mark

14 What change should be made in sentence 12?

Ⓕ change ***One*** to **Several**

Ⓖ change ***are*** to **is**

Ⓗ change ***shopping*** to **shoping**

Ⓘ change ***bags*** to **Bags**

15 What change should be made in sentence 13?

Ⓐ change ***problemes*** to **problems**

Ⓑ remove the comma after ***face***

Ⓒ remove the quotation mark before ***there***

Ⓓ change ***continue*** to **continues**

Name ______________________ Date ______________

Writing to Narrate

Read the prompt and plan your response.

Most people have faced an interesting problem that they had to solve.

Think about an interesting problem that someone might solve.

Now write a story about a character who solves that problem.

Planning Page

Use this space to make your notes before you begin writing. The writing on this page will NOT be scored.

Name ________________ Date ________________

Begin writing your response here. The writing on this page and the next page WILL be scored.

Name ______________________ Date ____________

Name ______________________ Date ______________

Reading Complex Text

Read the poem "The Iron Horse" and the article "On Track." As you read, stop and answer each question. Use evidence from the poem and article to support your answers.

The Iron Horse

I was born in the 1800s,
Even then turning heads.
I cross the land with unmatched speed,
Surpassing all my fellow steed.

But when I come, you barely see,
I sneak around with bended knee,
Then race even with the wind,
And chase the gusts till they disband.

Swifter than a brook can babble,
Where past and present come unraveled,
I leave all memory in a ditch,
And hurtle past without a hitch.

The iron horse is what they call me,
Coal, my food. Wheels, my feet.
I take in young and take in old,
And carry them through the heat and cold.

1. Pick a line from the section above that gives you a clue that the "the iron horse" is a train. Explain how this line supports the idea that it is a train.

____

____

____

Name ____________________ Date __________

From north to south, and east to west,
With rhythms strong and heaving chest,
I lurch around the mountain's back,
Peering up and down the track,
Then neighing loud as I descend,
I settle down among my friends.

2 Who is the narrator of this poem?

____

____

____

On Track

Did you ever think about how many stories, songs, and poems are about trains? You can probably think of a few right now. Given all of the storybooks and songs about trains, somebody might think children were the only people interested in trains.

When trains and railroads first appeared in the United States in the 1800s, they fascinated everybody. They were unlike anything ever seen before. Before trains, the only way to travel across land was on foot or by horse. Neither cars nor airplanes had been invented. A 100-mile journey from New York to Philadelphia, with two horses pulling a carriage, took three days. By train the same trip suddenly took three hours. Trains truly changed the way that people lived.

Name ______________________ Date ____________

3 How did trains change the way that people traveled?

____

____

____

Alongside the story of how railroads changed America is another story. It is the story of who built the railroads and how they did it. Thousands of railroad workers were immigrants. They came from Ireland, China, Mexico, and Japan seeking a better life. Many others were African American. They worked long hours for little pay. They worked in harsh weather and treacherous conditions. They dug tunnels through mountains and under rivers. They built bridges across rivers and gorges. They worked in snow up to their waists and in deserts with little water. Many did not survive the brutal work. But the work did not stop until the railroads crisscrossed the entire country.

Railroads changed both city life and country life. Now you could transport enough food from the country to feed a large city. You could carry enough wood and other supplies to build many houses. Farms also got bigger. Farmers could now transport the food they grew to many people both across the country and around the world. Trains carried the coal to heat the cities, run the factories, and fuel the trains themselves. They still do many of these things today.

Name ______________________ Date ____________

4. Tell one way that the poem compares a train and a horse. Then tell one way that the article compares a train and a horse.

____

____

____

____

____

Name ______________________ Date ____________

Reading and Analyzing Text

Read the story "Being Good" before answering Numbers 1 through 18.

Being Good

Walter's brother, Morgan, was a star athlete. He was a great runner, a superb swimmer, and a fine baseball player. People who saw Morgan run, swim, and throw a baseball all said the same thing, "He's amazing. He makes it look so easy!" Of course, a person who makes something look easy has usually worked hard at it. Morgan was that type of person. He practiced every single day.

Walter admired his brother's ability to play sports and wanted to do what Morgan could do. He wanted to run like the wind, swim like a shark, and swing a bat like . . . Morgan.

Two things stood in the way of Walter's success, though. The first was that Walter didn't enjoy sports all that much because he wasn't very good at them. The second was that he liked to spend his free time reading and writing stories. How would he find time to become good at running, swimming, and baseball?

In spite of these things, Walter announced to his family during dinner one night that he wanted to become good at sports. "I'm surprised to hear you say that. I didn't think you were interested in sports," said Mom when she heard the unexpected news. Dad looked at Walter with disbelief, and Morgan put down his glass of milk.

"You have to practice every day to be good, Walter," said Morgan. "How will you find the time, with your busy schedule?" Morgan continued, "My advice is to keep doing what you do well, which is writing stories."

Hearing this made Walter feel even more determined to prove himself in sports. He would work hard to succeed, and then people would praise him in the same way they praised Morgan.

The next day, Walter stayed after school and ran ten laps around the track. That night, after he finished his homework, he practiced swinging a baseball bat in the backyard. The following day was Saturday. When

Walter woke up, his legs and arms were sore, but he went to the pool with Morgan anyway. He swam for an hour. Walter was so tired that he took a long nap when they got back home. When he woke up, he went running again and practiced throwing a baseball.

The next week, Walter did the same thing. His body ached all over, and he was tired most of the time. Mom and Dad were worried that he was trying too hard, so they had a talk with Walter. "Is this what you *really* want to do?" asked Dad.

"Well, it's not much fun," Walter admitted. "Morgan seems to enjoy sports a lot more than I do, but I want to be as good as he is."

"You're already good at something," said Mom. "You're a creative storyteller and an outstanding writer! You're already a champion, so why do you want to be good at something you don't enjoy?"

"People don't seem to care that much about writers," said Walter. "Do you ever see a photograph of a writer on a cereal box?"

"Walter," Dad said, "people do care about good writers, and besides, you don't have to be good at everything."

Walter thought about what his parents were saying and realized that they were right. He decided to give up trying to be as good as Morgan at sports. The decision gave him a feeling of great relief, and he could almost feel his muscles get a little less sore.

A week later, Walter wrote a school essay about trying to be something he's not. Walter's teacher thought the essay was excellent and asked his permission to send the essay to a student magazine. Walter's writing appeared in the magazine a few months later. His classmates and family were very proud of him.

"I wish I could write as well as you can," said Morgan, smiling at his brother. "You make it look so easy!"

Name ______________________ Date __________

Now answer Numbers 1 through 18. Base your answers on the story "Being Good."

1. Read this sentence from the story.

   Walter's brother, Morgan, was a star athlete.

   What does the word *athlete* mean in the sentence above?

   Ⓐ someone who plays sports

   Ⓑ someone who throws a ball

   Ⓒ someone who does well in school

   Ⓓ someone who practices every day

2. How does Walter like to spend his free time?

   Ⓕ playing baseball

   Ⓖ taking photographs

   Ⓗ running and swimming

   Ⓘ reading and writing stories

3. Read this sentence from the story.

   Dad looked at Walter with disbelief, and Morgan put down his glass of milk.

   What does the word *disbelief* mean in the sentence above?

   Ⓐ trying to believe

   Ⓑ someone who believes

   Ⓒ the opposite of believing

   Ⓓ something to be believed

Name ______________________ Date ____________

4 Which of the following can the reader tell from the story?

- Ⓕ Being good at sports requires practice.
- Ⓖ Most people are only good at one sport.
- Ⓗ A person who tries hard enough will become good at sports.
- Ⓘ Being good at sports is more important than being a good writer.

5 Read this sentence from the story.

Morgan continued, "My advice is to keep doing what you do well, which is writing stories."

What does the word *advice* mean in the sentence above?

- Ⓐ a guess about what will happen
- Ⓑ a wish for something to happen
- Ⓒ an opinion about what should happen
- Ⓓ an idea about what has already happened

6 Why does Walter want to be good at sports?

- Ⓕ so he can make new friends
- Ⓖ so he can have a healthy body
- Ⓗ so he can get praise from others
- Ⓘ so he can write about being an athlete

Name ____________________ Date ____________

7 Read this sentence from the story.

Hearing this made Walter feel even more determined to prove himself in sports.

What does the word *prove* mean in the sentence above?

Ⓐ challenge

Ⓑ hide

Ⓒ show

Ⓓ struggle

8 Read this sentence from the story.

When Walter woke up, his legs and arms were sore, but he went to the pool with Morgan anyway.

What does the word *sore* mean in the sentence above?

Ⓕ angry

Ⓖ hurting

Ⓗ sail high in the air

Ⓘ rise to a high level

9 What can the reader BEST tell about Morgan from the story?

Ⓐ He is not as fast as everyone says he is.

Ⓑ He respects Walter for his own talents.

Ⓒ He doesn't believe Walter can be good at sports.

Ⓓ He thinks his talent is more important than Walter's.

Name ______________________ Date ______________

10 Why are Mom and Dad worried about Walter?

Ⓕ He is missing his friends.

Ⓖ He is not good at writing.

Ⓗ He is not helping enough at home.

Ⓘ He is trying too hard to be good at sports.

11 Read this sentence from the story.

"You're already a champion, so why do you want to be good at something you don't enjoy?"

What does the word *champion* mean in the sentence above?

Ⓐ a person who wants to be an athlete

Ⓑ a person who wants to be good at something

Ⓒ a person who is among the best at something

Ⓓ a person who is the very first to do something

12 Read this sentence from the story.

"Do you ever see a photograph of a writer on a cereal box?"

What does the word *photograph* mean in the sentence above?

Ⓕ a type of award

Ⓖ a type of picture

Ⓗ a type of writing

Ⓘ a type of magazine

Name ______________________ Date ____________

13 How does Walter change by the end of the story?

Ⓐ He gives up his plan to become good at sports.

Ⓑ He decides to practice only one sport every day.

Ⓒ He becomes more determined to be good at sports.

Ⓓ He decides to write about the sports he enjoys most.

14 Which of Walter's abilities does Morgan value MOST?

Ⓕ reading

Ⓖ running

Ⓗ swimming

Ⓘ writing

15 Read this sentence from the story.

Walter thought about what his parents were saying and realized that they were right.

What is the LAST syllable in the word *Walter*?

Ⓐ er

Ⓑ ter

Ⓒ lter

Ⓓ alter

Name ______________________ Date ____________

16 Read this sentence from the story.

The decision gave him a feeling of great relief, and he could almost feel his muscles get a little less sore.

What is the LAST syllable in the word *decision*?

Ⓕ on

Ⓖ ion

Ⓗ sion

Ⓘ ision

17 Read this sentence from the story.

Walter's teacher thought the essay was excellent and asked his permission to send the essay to a student magazine.

What shows the correct way to divide the word *excellent* into syllables?

Ⓐ exc • ell • ent

Ⓑ ex • cell • ent

Ⓒ exc • ell • ent

Ⓓ ex • cel • lent

18 Read this sentence from the story.

Walter's teacher thought the essay was excellent and asked his permission to send the essay to a student magazine.

Which word has the same sound as the underlined letter in *magazine*?

Ⓕ about

Ⓖ aim

Ⓗ almost

Ⓘ arch

Name ______________________ Date ____________

Read the article "A Whole Other Country" before answering Numbers 19 through 35.

A Whole Other Country

Some people who have never visited Texas think the land is the same throughout the state. Some think the state is all desert filled with cactus. Others think it is an endless plain. Both are partly right. Texas has many deserts and plains, but those are just two types of the impressive land features found there. Texas also has mountains, forests, beaches, and canyons. The state is so large and so varied that some people use the expression "a whole other country" to describe it.

You can probably recognize the outline of Texas. Its shape is partly formed by water. In the north, the Red River forms the border between Oklahoma and Texas. The Sabine River separates Texas and Louisiana in the east. The Gulf of Mexico forms the southeast border of the state. The Rio Grande divides Texas from Mexico in the west and the south.

If you look at a map of Texas, you will see that eastern Texas has mostly plains and a few small hills. Western Texas has plains, hills, and mountains. The state has four main natural regions, or areas. The four regions are the Gulf Coastal Plain, the Central Plains, the High Plains, and the Mountains and Basins. The landscape of each region differs from that of the others.

Gulf Coastal Plain

The Gulf Coastal Plain region covers the eastern and southern part of Texas. It is the largest region in the state. The Gulf Coastal Plain runs along the Gulf of Mexico. The land here is mostly low and flat. Part of this region is tropical. You'll find miles of sandy beaches here. The region also reaches inland, away from the coast, for about 250 miles. Fields of vegetables and fruits grow to the west of the coast.

Central Plains

As you move away from the Gulf of Mexico, the land begins to rise. The Central Plains region is in the north-central part of the state.

Name ________________________ Date ____________

It has rolling hills and valleys. Many Texans call this region the Hill Country. Cattle and sheep graze on the grassy land there.

For hundreds of years, ancient rivers and streams shaped the land of the Central Plains. As you go farther west, there are forests of oak and hickory trees. Many different crops grow in this region.

High Plains

The High Plains are west of the Central Plains and are also part of the Great Plains of the United States. The land here is high and flat and looks something like a table. Parts of the High Plains are marked by long walls of steep cliffs and slopes. The southern and eastern parts are hilly. Many legends about rough, tough Texas cowhands are from the High Plains.

Mountains and Basins

This region is in western Texas. The land here is high, dry, and often rugged. The soil is dry and rocky. There are many small mountain ranges and dramatic cliffs in this region of Texas. These mountains are part of the Rocky Mountains, which stretch from Mexico to Canada. The highest peak in Texas is Guadalupe Peak. It rises nearly 9,000 feet above sea level.

A basin is land shaped like a bowl that has higher ground around it. In this region, the basins are parts of large deserts. You can visit Big Bend National Park in the Mountains and Basins region. You can also gaze at stars through a huge telescope at the McDonald Observatory in the Davis Mountains, which are also in this region.

The Land Called Texas

The state of Texas is varied and vast. It's no wonder that for centuries people have been drawn to this land. That may be why some call it a whole other country!

Name ______________________ Date ______________

Now answer Numbers 19 through 35. Base your answers on the article "A Whole Other Country."

19 Read this sentence from the article.

Others think it is an endless plain.

What does the word *plain* mean in the sentence above?

Ⓐ a flat area

Ⓑ easy to see

Ⓒ not mixed with anything

Ⓓ a vehicle that flies in the sky

20 Read this sentence from the article.

The state is so large and so varied that some people use the expression "a whole other country" to describe it.

What does the word *expression* mean in the sentence above?

Ⓕ a familiar saying

Ⓖ a symbol for an idea

Ⓗ a person's first language

Ⓘ a statement that is untrue

21 Which of the following partly forms the outline of Texas?

Ⓐ hills

Ⓑ water

Ⓒ plains

Ⓓ mountains

Name ______________________ Date ______________

22 Read this sentence from the article.

The Sabine River separates Texas and Louisiana in the east.

Which word has the same sound as the underlined letter in *separates*?

Ⓕ acorn

Ⓖ actor

Ⓗ although

Ⓘ around

23 Read this sentence from the article.

The landscape of each region differs from that of the others.

What does the word *landscape* mean in the sentence above?

Ⓐ land that is owned

Ⓑ broad, flat-topped land

Ⓒ the landforms of a region

Ⓓ land that has not been settled

24 Which of these shaped the land in the Central Plains region?

Ⓕ rivers and streams

Ⓖ the Gulf of Mexico

Ⓗ the Rocky Mountains

Ⓘ grazing cattle and sheep

Name ______________________ Date ______________

25 Read this sentence from the article.

Cattle and sheep graze on the grassy land there.

What is the correct way to divide the word *cattle* into syllables?

Ⓐ ca • ttle

Ⓑ ca • tt • le

Ⓒ cat • tle

Ⓓ catt • le

26 Study this box.

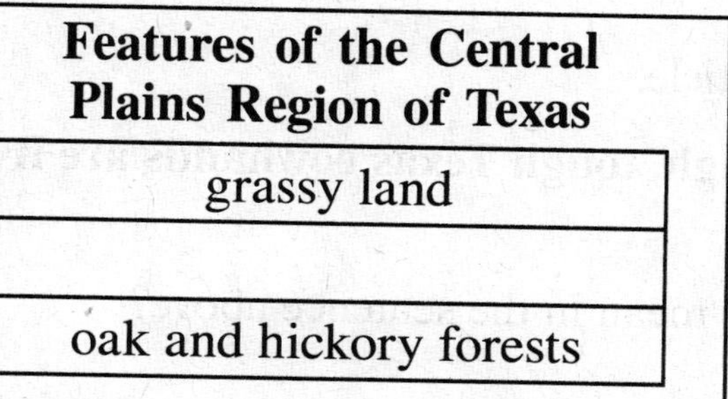

Features of the Central Plains Region of Texas
grassy land
oak and hickory forests

Which information belongs in the empty box?

Ⓕ steep cliffs

Ⓖ rolling hills

Ⓗ low, flat land

Ⓘ sandy beaches

Name ______________________ Date ____________

27 Read this sentence from the article.

Many legends about rough, tough Texas cowhands are from the High Plains.

Which word has the same sound as the underlined part of the word *tough*?

Ⓐ caught

Ⓑ ouch

Ⓒ such

Ⓓ watch

28 Read this sentence from the article.

Many legends about rough, tough Texas cowhands are from the High Plains.

What does the word *cowhands* mean in the sentence above?

Ⓕ fenced areas for cattle

Ⓖ ropes used for catching cattle

Ⓗ people who take care of cattle

Ⓘ ranches where cattle are raised

29 In what region of Texas can deserts be found?

Ⓐ Gulf Coastal Plain

Ⓑ Central Plains

Ⓒ High Plains

Ⓓ Mountains and Basins

Name _______________ Date ___________

30 Read this sentence from the article.

There are many small mountain ranges and dramatic cliffs in this region of Texas.

What does the word *dramatic* mean in the sentence above?

Ⓕ unusual

Ⓖ dangerous

Ⓗ causing wonder or awe

Ⓘ having a variety of forms

31 Read this sentence from the article.

The highest peak in Texas is Guadalupe Peak.

What does the word *peak* mean in the sentence above?

Ⓐ small hill

Ⓑ desert floor

Ⓒ grassy plain

Ⓓ mountain top

32 Read this sentence from the article.

You can also gaze at stars through a huge telescope at the McDonald Observatory in the Davis Mountains, which are also in this region.

In the sentence above, the word *telescope* means an instrument that can help you see which types of objects?

Ⓕ small objects

Ⓖ nearby objects

Ⓗ moving objects

Ⓘ far-away objects

33 What is this article MOSTLY about?

Ⓐ how the mountains and valleys in Texas were formed

Ⓑ how the Texas plains differ from the deserts in West Texas

Ⓒ the variety of native plants and animals that can be found in Texas

Ⓓ the different regions and landscapes that make up the state of Texas

34 According to the article, why do people often refer to Texas as "a whole other country"?

Ⓕ It shares its southern border with another country.

Ⓖ The state is so large and has so many different regions.

Ⓗ The land differs so greatly from the rest of the United States.

Ⓘ Many people mistake it for another country when they see it on a map.

35 Which sentence from the article states a FACT?

Ⓐ "Some think the state is all desert filled with cactus."

Ⓑ "Others think it is an endless plain."

Ⓒ "The state has four main natural regions, or areas."

Ⓓ "It's no wonder that for centuries people have been drawn to this land."

Name ______________________ Date ____________

Revising and Editing

Read the introduction and the story "Mrs. Cantu's Gift" before answering Numbers 1 through 5.

Mita wrote this story about a special neighborhood event. Read her story and think about the changes she should make.

Mrs. Cantu's Gift

(1) Our neighborhood is a large, friendly, and lively community. (2) More than 30 families live here. (3) Last month, something wonderful happened in our neighborhood. (4) We created a community garden! (5) Mrs. Cantu thought on the idea. (6) She has a backyard vegetable garden that everyone admires, and next to the house is a large piece of land that is hers.

(7) "Not everyone has room for a garden," said Mrs. Cantu, "so let's build a garden that will benefit everyone in the neighborhood." (8) Mrs. Cantu taught music at our school until she retired last year.

(9) People in the community helped dig the garden, and Mrs. Cantu advised us about what to plant. (10) On Saturday, Mar. 3, everyone gathered at the garden to plant and water vegetable seeds. (11) Then we had a huge celebration. (12) Mrs. Cantu made a speech, and we ate sandwiches, apples and carrots for lunch.

(13) Families in the neighborhood will take turns caring for the garden and we will all share in the results. (14) What a great gift to the community!

Name ____________________ Date ____________

Now answer Numbers 1 through 5. Base your answers on the changes Mita should make.

1. What change should be made in sentence 5?

   Ⓐ add a comma after ***Mrs. Cantu***

   Ⓑ change ***thought*** to **thinked**

   Ⓒ change ***on*** to **of**

   Ⓓ change the period to a question mark

2. What change should be made in sentence 10?

   Ⓕ remove the comma after ***Saturday***

   Ⓖ change ***Mar.*** to **March**

   Ⓗ change ***gathered*** to **gatherred**

   Ⓘ add a comma after ***garden***

3. What change should be made in sentence 12?

   Ⓐ change ***made*** to **make**

   Ⓑ remove the comma after ***speech***

   Ⓒ add a comma after ***apples***

   Ⓓ change ***for*** to **in**

4. What change should be made in sentence 13?

   Ⓕ change ***Families*** to **Family's**

   Ⓖ change ***in*** to **on**

   Ⓗ add a comma after ***garden***

   Ⓘ change ***share*** to **sharing**

Name ______________________ Date ____________

5 Which sentence does NOT belong in this story?

Ⓐ sentence 2

Ⓑ sentence 3

Ⓒ sentence 4

Ⓓ sentence 8

Name ______________________ Date ____________

Read the introduction and the story "The Wild World Outside My Window" before answering Numbers 6 through 10.

Nicky wrote this story about an experience that she had. Read her story and think about the changes she should make.

The Wild World Outside My Window

(1) A week after we moved to Richmond Virginia, I caught the flu. (2) Having the flu isn't fun, because your body feels tired and achy. (3) To make it even worse, I had to stay in bed for several days.

(4) The first day, I read three books, but by the second day, I was bored silly. (5) Then an interesting thing happened. (6) I noticed something flash past my window. (7) I looked outside and saw a strange bird with a long neck and long legs perched on a rock in our yard!

(8) "Thats a blue heron," Mom said. (9) "They wade in shallow water and catch fish with there sharp beaks." (10) Then, Mom and me watched a squirrel chase another squirrel around the trunk of our walnut tree. (11) Later, I saw three black crows hopping from tree to tree and six gray birds hunting for worms on the ground. (12) Then, a brown rabbit with a white tail hopped out of the bushes and sniffed at a pile of leaves.

(13) Staying in bed wasn't so bad after all. (14) The squirrels, birds, and rabbit kept me from getting bored and showed me an exciting world right outside my bedroom window.

Now answer Numbers 6 through 10. Base your answers on the changes Nicky should make.

6. What change should be made in sentence 1?
   - Ⓕ change ***we*** to **us**
   - Ⓖ add a comma after ***Richmond***
   - Ⓗ remove the comma after ***Virginia***
   - Ⓘ change ***flu*** to **flew**

7. Which sentence could BEST be added after sentence 7?
   - Ⓐ I ate soup that Mom made.
   - Ⓑ I read my book for a while.
   - Ⓒ I called Mom into my room.
   - Ⓓ I saw an unusual bird with long legs.

8. What change should be made in sentence 8?
   - Ⓕ change ***Thats*** to **That's**
   - Ⓖ change ***blue*** to **blew**
   - Ⓗ remove the comma after ***heron***
   - Ⓘ change ***said*** to **say**

Name ______________________ Date ____________

9. What change should be made in sentence 9?

Ⓐ change ***shallow*** to **shalow**

Ⓑ add a comma after ***fish***

Ⓒ change ***there*** to **their**

Ⓓ change ***beaks*** to **bekes**

10. What change should be made in sentence 10?

Ⓕ change ***Mom*** to **mom**

Ⓖ change ***me*** to **I**

Ⓗ add a comma after ***watched***

Ⓘ change ***our*** to **are**

Name ______________________ Date ____________

Read the introduction and the article "From Planet to Ice Ball" before answering Numbers 11 through 15.

Hamid wrote this article about Pluto. Read his article and think about the changes he should make.

From Planet to Ice Ball

(1) Pluto used to be one of the nine planets in our solar system but now it's just a small ice ball. (2) "There are finally, officially, eight planets in the solar system" says a scientist who studies the stars. (3) How does a planet get voted out of the club?

(4) Scientists made this decision at a meeting in 2006. (5) They voted and decided that Pluto is not a true planet. (6) First, though, the scientists had to agree in exactly what makes an object a planet. (7) Before 2006, they didn't have an official definition of a "planet."

(8) Now, scientists say that to be a planet, an object must meet three requirements. First, the object must orbit, or journey, around the sun. (9) Second the object must be large enough to have a round shape from the force of its gravity. (10) Third, the object must clear a path along its journey around the sun.

(11) While Pluto meets the first two requirements, it has comets and other things in its path. (12) Pluto is now called a

Name ______________________ Date ______________

dwarf planet. (13) Even though it has been downgraded, it still enjois a special place in many people's hearts.

Now answer Numbers 11 through 15. Base your answers on the changes Hamid should make.

11 What change should be made in sentence 1?

- Ⓐ change ***Pluto*** to **pluto**
- Ⓑ add a comma after ***system***
- Ⓒ change ***it's*** to **its**
- Ⓓ add a comma after ***small***

12 What change should be made in sentence 2?

- Ⓕ change ***there*** to **their**
- Ⓖ add a comma after ***system***
- Ⓗ add a quotation mark after ***scientist***
- Ⓘ change ***studies*** to **study**

13 What change should be made in sentence 6?

- Ⓐ remove the comma after ***though***
- Ⓑ change ***had*** to **have**
- Ⓒ change ***in*** to **on**
- Ⓓ change ***an*** to **a**

Name ______________________ Date ____________

14 What change should be made in sentence 9?

Ⓕ add a comma after ***Second***

Ⓖ change ***large*** to **larje**

Ⓗ add a comma after ***enough***

Ⓘ change ***force*** to **forced**

15 What change should be made in sentence 13?

Ⓐ add a comma after ***though***

Ⓑ change ***enjois*** to **enjoys**

Ⓒ change ***in*** to **on**

Ⓓ change ***people's*** to **peoples'**

STOP

Name ____________________ Date ____________

Writing to Inform

Read the prompt and plan your response.

Most people have a sport or game that they enjoy.

Think about how a sport or game that you enjoy is played.

Now write to explain how to play a sport or game that you enjoy.

Planning Page

Use this space to make your notes before you begin writing. The writing on this page will NOT be scored.

Name ______________________ Date ____________

Begin writing your response here. The writing on this page and the next page WILL be scored.

Name ____________________ Date __________

Writing to Inform

Name ______________________ Date ____________

Reading Complex Text

Read the articles "A Look at Volcanoes: From the Inside Out" and "The Eruption of Mount Vesuvius." As you read, stop and answer each question. Use evidence from the articles to support your answers.

A Look at Volcanoes: From the Inside Out

Have you ever tried shaking a bottle of soda and then suddenly removed the cap? All the liquid and little bubbles inside the bottle instantly shoot up out of the bottle. They make a big explosion that is not always easy to clean up.

When a volcano erupts, something similar happens on a much larger scale. Gases inside the earth expand. They push out large masses of lava, or liquid rock. The lava shoots up through an opening at the top of a mountain. In this way, the earth is like a giant soda bottle. It is not always the solid rock it appears to be.

Volcanoes are found all over the world. They have shaped the planet's mountains, plains, and plateaus. Volcanoes formed more than 80 percent of the earth's surface, above and below the sea.

Scientists say that the earth's surface is made up of a number of shifting plates. When the plates crash into each other, volcanoes can form. Most volcanoes are located along the boundaries of these plates. The boundaries are where the two plates collide.

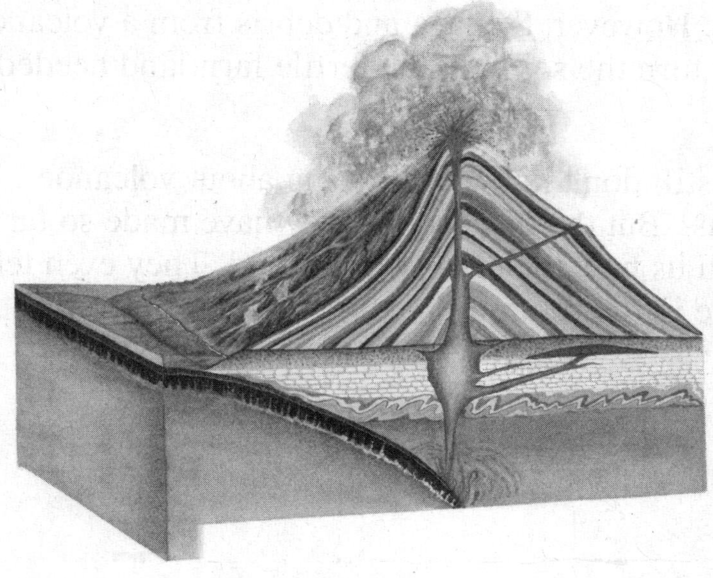

Name ______________________ Date ____________

1 What information from the article does the illustration show?

____

____

____

Much volcanic material comes from below the plates in the earth's middle layer. This layer is called the mantle. Temperatures there get very high. The heat can cause solid rock to turn to liquid and form magma. When a volcano erupts, the magma breaks through the earth's surface. Then it is known by a different name, lava. When a volcano goes through an active period, the lava that comes out and cools may build up to form a hill or mountain.

People did not always understand volcanoes the way scientists do today. They once thought volcanoes were supernatural forces. In ancient Rome, they believed volcanoes were the chimneys of a god named Vulcan.

That is where the word *volcano* comes from. In myths, Vulcan was a blacksmith. He used his furnace to forge thunderbolts for Jupiter, the king of all the gods, and weapons for Mars, the god of war.

Volcanoes can be destructive. They can bury whole cities in burning lava and ashes. However, the lava and debris from a volcano also have benefits. They turn the soil into the fertile farmland needed to sustain human life.

Geologists still don't know everything about volcanoes. They still have many questions. But the discoveries they have made so far give us great clues. They tell us how the earth was formed. They even tell us what it might look like in the future.

Name ______________________ Date ______________

2 How did volcanoes get their name?

____

____

____

The Eruption of Mount Vesuvius

Nearly 2,000 years ago, in a small town in southern Italy, a teenage boy was living at the home of his uncle. It was the afternoon of August 24 in the year 79 AD. The boy's mother called his attention to an unusual cloud in the distance. This cloud, said the boy, "rose to a great height on a sort of trunk." It "then split off into branches." In some places "it looked white, elsewhere blotched and dirty."

The boy's uncle was a navy officer in charge of a fleet of ships. He was also a scientist interested in unusual events in nature. He decided to set off at once on one of his ships. He wanted to get a closer view of the cloud. He asked the boy, who was also his student, if he wanted to join him. But the boy thought better of it. "I replied that I preferred to go on with my studies."

It turned out that the cloud was not a cloud at all. It was the erupting volcano of Mount Vesuvius. It filled the sky for miles with intensely hot lava and ashes. This debris would rain down upon the surrounding cities and countryside for two days.

Name ______________________ Date ____________

3 Use the information in the first article to explain what is causing the eruption of Mount Vesuvius in the second article.

____

____

____

The uncle soon heard of the dangers into which he was heading. Yet, instead of turning back, he bravely kept going. He was hoping to rescue some of the many people living near the volcano. As the boy described it, "Ashes were already falling, hotter and thicker as the ships drew near."

Those ashes buried the two cities of Pompeii and Herculaneum. It was not until 1748 that the cities were re-discovered. The boy's uncle died in those ashes. Even though the boy did not understand volcanoes the way scientists do today, he would go on to write a vivid account of that day.

4 What is one way in which both articles are SIMILAR? What is one way in which they are DIFFERENT?

____

____

____

____

____

Name ______________________________ Date ______________

Donavan's Word Jar

Answer Numbers 1 through 10. Base your answers on the novel *Donavan's Word Jar.*

1. What does Donavan collect?

   Ⓐ buttons

   Ⓑ coins

   Ⓒ marbles

   Ⓓ words

2. In Chapter 2, what does Donavan use the dictionary to learn?

   Ⓕ how pincers are used

   Ⓖ what pincers look like

   Ⓗ how to spell the word *pincers*

   Ⓘ when the first pincers were made

3. In Chapter 2, what does Donavan learn about words?

   Ⓐ They can only be written.

   Ⓑ They are always easy to spell.

   Ⓒ They can be found everywhere.

   Ⓓ They are always hard to understand

4. In Chapter 3, what is Donavan's problem?

   Ⓕ He is late for school.

   Ⓖ He cannot find his dictionary.

   Ⓗ He cannot fit any more words in his jar.

   Ⓘ He needs to keep his sister out of his collection.

Name ______________________ Date __________

5 Who suggests that Donavan start his own dictionary?

Ⓐ his sister

Ⓑ his father

Ⓒ his mother

Ⓓ his teacher

6 What is the setting for Chapter 4?

Ⓕ Dad's new shop

Ⓖ Donavan's house

Ⓗ Grandma's house

Ⓘ Donavan's school

7 Which of the following sentences helps the reader visualize that Nikki is sick?

Ⓐ "On her lap sat a large box of tissues."

Ⓑ "Donavan always had to tell Nikki things."

Ⓒ "She laughed and asked, 'Donnie, is that a real word?'"

Ⓓ "Donavan opened the door to Nikki's room and peeped in."

8 In Chapter 5, why does Donavan make Nikki promise to give back the word she picks out of his jar?

Ⓕ He knows she cannot read.

Ⓖ He is worried she will keep it.

Ⓗ He is afraid he will catch her cold.

Ⓘ He does not want her to draw on the paper.

Name ____________________ Date __________

9. In Chapter 6, who does Donavan go to see for help with his problem?

Ⓐ his father
Ⓑ his friend
Ⓒ his teacher
Ⓓ his grandmother

10. What does Grandma do when she sees Donavan's word jar?

Ⓕ She feels proud of him for his collection.
Ⓖ She thinks collecting words is silly.
Ⓗ She gets angry that he wastes his time collecting words.
Ⓘ She tells him he should share his word collection with others.

STOP

Name _______________________ Date ____________

Jake Drake, Know-It-All

Answer Numbers 1 through 10. Base your answers on the novel *Jake Drake, Know-It-All.*

1. What is Jake's favorite thing to do?

   Ⓐ read mysteries
   Ⓑ use a computer
   Ⓒ cook good things to eat
   Ⓓ play sports with his friends

2. Which word does Jake use to describe himself?

   Ⓕ awkward
   Ⓖ greedy
   Ⓗ lazy
   Ⓘ smart

3. Which of the following sentences from Chapter 2 helps the reader visualize what Mrs. Karp looks like?

   Ⓐ "I thought maybe he worked for a circus."
   Ⓑ "Every kid in school knows how loud she can yell."
   Ⓒ "He was wearing a yellow sport coat and a purple tie with green polka dots."
   Ⓓ "But standing up on the stage that morning in a green dress, she looked like a giant piece of celery."

Name ______________________ Date ____________

4 Which detail shows that Mr. Cordo is scared to talk to the students?

Ⓕ He is sweating.

Ⓖ He thanks Mrs. Karp.

Ⓗ He says he is glad to be there.

Ⓘ He has to pull the microphone down.

5 How does Mr. Cordo get the students excited about the science fair?

Ⓐ He tells them they will be on TV.

Ⓑ He promises to give them a grand prize.

Ⓒ He offers them a job at his store.

Ⓓ He says he will give them money for each project that is entered.

6 What is Chapter 3 mostly about?

Ⓕ how to make a rocket

Ⓖ the rules for the science fair

Ⓗ how a computer game works

Ⓘ the things Jake talks to his family about

7 In Chapter 5, what happens when Jake's dad suggests that he build a rocket?

Ⓐ Jake asks if he could go to the library to do some research.

Ⓑ Jake gets excited because he thinks the judges will like that idea.

Ⓒ Jake says he does not like the idea because it will be too much work.

Ⓓ Jake tells him he cannot make anything that burns, smokes, or explodes.

Name ____________________ Date ______________

8. In Chapter 6, what does Jake pick for his project?
   - Ⓕ building a rocket
   - Ⓖ watching how ants live
   - Ⓗ making an electromagnet
   - Ⓘ growing different kinds of plants

9. In Chapter 7, how does Jake show he is clever?
   - Ⓐ He keeps the secret that his sister Abby broke a statue.
   - Ⓑ He makes a list of all the things that are in his junk drawer.
   - Ⓒ He lets other students see him with things that have nothing to do with his project.
   - Ⓓ He lets Kevin stand behind him when he gets in line to turn in his permission slip.

10. Who wins first place for the third grade at the science fair?
   - Ⓕ Jake
   - Ⓖ Kevin
   - Ⓗ Marsha
   - Ⓘ Pete

Name ______________________ Date ____________

Capoeira

Answer Numbers 1 through 10. Base your answers on the novel *Capoeira*.

1. According to legend, who created capoeira?
   - Ⓐ African slaves
   - Ⓑ Brazilian children
   - Ⓒ Native Americans
   - Ⓓ Portuguese explorers

2. Why did capoeira players use nicknames in the late nineteenth century?
   - Ⓕ The game was illegal.
   - Ⓖ It made the game more fun.
   - Ⓗ The game was only for adults.
   - Ⓘ It allowed the children to practice their Portuguese.

3. While playing, which part of the capoeiristas can touch the floor?
   - Ⓐ their back and sides
   - Ⓑ their shoulders and elbows
   - Ⓒ their hands, feet, and head
   - Ⓓ their arms, legs, and stomach

4. What can the reader conclude about capoeira moves?
   - Ⓕ They are never used in fighting.
   - Ⓖ They can only be done by children.
   - Ⓗ They look like the thing for which they are named.
   - Ⓘ They are always named after some kind of living thing.

Name ______________________ Date ______________

5 Which of the following sentences states an opinion?

Ⓐ "The ginga is a springboard for the many movements that follow."

Ⓑ "When two players start a game they face each other and step from side to side and forward and back in a kind of dance."

Ⓒ "The object of the game is to put one's opponent in a position where he or she could be taken down with a sweep, kick, or blow."

Ⓓ "Capoeiristas are playful and respectful as they move in continuous sequences from attack to defense and back to attack."

6 What must people who play capoeira be?

Ⓕ very tall

Ⓖ good singers

Ⓗ able to run fast

Ⓘ able to move easily

7 Which of the following sentences helps the reader visualize what a berimbau is?

Ⓐ "The berimbau is used to direct the capoeira games."

Ⓑ "After teaching the students the song, Malandro begins to play an instrument called a berimbau."

Ⓒ "The berimbau is a long wood bow with a steel wire and a hollowed-out gourd near the bottom."

Ⓓ "In nineteenth-century Brazil berimbaus were also used by peddlers to announce their arrival in town."

8 What do two players at Mandinga Academey do before they play the game?

Ⓕ They hold hands.

Ⓖ They sing a song.

Ⓗ They clap loudly.

Ⓘ They hug each other.

9 Which word tells the reader that this sentence states an opinion?

The players have fun and try to make their moves graceful, like a dance.

Ⓐ dance

Ⓑ fun

Ⓒ like

Ⓓ moves

10 Which word from the book is used to state an opinion?

Ⓕ cities

Ⓖ discover

Ⓗ practice

Ⓘ thrill